MW01680406

STAAR Grade 7 Writing Assessment Secrets

Study Guide

Your Key to Exam Success

STAAR Test Review for the

State of Texas Assessments of Academic Readiness

Written and edited by the Mometrix Exam Secrets Test Prep Team
Printed in the United States of America

Dear Future Exam Success Story:

Congratulations on your purchase of our study guide. Our goal in writing our study guide was to cover the content on the test, as well as provide insight into typical test taking mistakes and how to overcome them.

Standardized tests are a key component of being successful, which only increases the importance of doing well in the high-pressure high-stakes environment of test day. How well you do on this test will have a significant impact on your future- and we have the research and practical advice to help you execute on test day.

The product you're reading now is designed to exploit weaknesses in the test itself, and help you avoid the most common errors test takers frequently make.

How to use this study guide

We don't want to waste your time. Our study guide is fast-paced and fluff-free. We suggest going through it a number of times, as repetition is an important part of learning new information and concepts.

First, read through the study guide completely to get a feel for the content and organization. Read the general success strategies first, and then proceed to the content sections. Each tip has been carefully selected for its effectiveness.

Second, read through the study guide again, and take notes in the margins and highlight those sections where you may have a particular weakness.

Finally, bring the manual with you on test day and study it before the exam begins.

Your success is our success

We would be delighted to hear about your success. Send us an email and tell us your story. Thanks for your business and we wish you continued success-

Sincerely,

Mometrix Test Preparation Team

TABLE OF CONTENTS

Writing Assessment

Purpose

A purpose is the reason that an author writes an article. There are many reasons to write articles; an author may want to express ideas, solve a problem, or inform a reader about something. An author may want to make a request or argue a point. An author may want to explain how something works or persuade a reader to do something. An author may want to entertain the reader or make the reader laugh out loud. An author may want to narrate the events of a story or report on something that has happened. There are many reasons that authors have for writing an article. It is important for the reader to understand what the author's purpose is while reading an article.

Example 1
Explain why the purpose of the passage below is to inform:

> Land turtles can be tiny enough to fit into a coat pocket or huge creatures that weigh over 500 pounds, and these giant turtles, or tortoises, often have shells that are more than four feet long. They nest in sand where they lay their eggs. Many of their offspring do not survive because they are eaten by scavengers. Those who do make it into the ocean may grow to maturity and then return to the very same beach to nest and lay their eggs.

This passage talks about land turtles and gives many details about what they look like and their lives. There is nothing in the passage that tries to persuade the reader and there are no statements of opinion in the passage at all. Instead all of the statements are facts and this is what a passage does that has as its purpose to inform. It states details or facts about a topic. This passage is not funny so it is not meant to amuse. The passage does not solve any problem either or request anything, nor does it narrate a story. That is why its purpose is to inform.

Example 2
Tell what purpose the passage below has:

> It seems clear to me that dogs have been man's best friend since prehistoric days. They have hunted with people all over the world, sometimes tracking lions, or retrieving birds, or cornering wild boars, or chasing foxes. When herdsmen herd their cows and sheep, dogs keep the animals in place. Dogs have led the blind, tracked down lost people, and pulled sleds in the Arctic. You can see that they have helped man for thousands of years.

The passage is about how dogs are man's best friend. It begins by making a statement that is a personal opinion. Then the author gives reasons for this opinion. The author tells the reader that dogs "have hunted with people all over the world" and that when "herdsmen herd their cows and sheep, dogs keep the animals in place" and that dogs "led the blind, tracked down lost people, and pulled sleds." The author is trying to persuade the reader that his statement is correct so the author gives reasons that support the author's opinion about dogs. This is the purpose of the passage.

Cohesive and coherent texts

Cohesive and coherent texts use many techniques. They organize ideas so that they flow from one to another. Each sentence should be logically linked to the next so that they form a "chain." Each sentence should help move the text forward. They should be organized in a way to help the reader understand the point of the article. Each paragraph should have a clear purpose. The paragraphs should be linked logically. The author should use effective transitions between sentences and paragraphs so the text flows naturally. The author should choose precise wording so that the writing is interesting and varied and the meaning is clear.

Literary devices

Literary devices are techniques that authors use to create artful modes of expression. Figurative language is one literary device. Figurative language allows the author to expand reality in a vivid way. Examples of figurative language are simile, metaphor, and personification. Similes compare things using the comparing words *like* or *as*. Metaphors compare things without using comparing words. Personification gives a thing or animal human traits. Another literary device is suspense. An author can build suspense in a story by using flashbacks. These allow the author to start the story at an exciting time and then tell what led up to it. Foreshadowing builds suspense too. It gives the reader hints about future events. Dialogue is another literary device. It allows the author to have the reader learn about characters from the words they speak.

<u>Figurative language</u>
Example: Explain which form of figurative language is used in the sentences below.
The counter sighed under the weight of all the dishes. It couldn't breathe. Everything was piled on top it and it felt like it wanted to scream and tell the chickens, beef, ham, and pies to get off.

The sentences say that the counter sighed and it couldn't breathe and that it wanted to scream. But these are things that counters cannot do. They cannot sigh or scream. These activities are something that people might do, so the author is using personification to make the writing more vivid. The author is giving this inanimate thing human traits or characteristics. This is not a simile because a simile compares two things by using the words *like* or *as*. This is not a metaphor either because two things are not being compared. The object is acting like a human and this is the definition of personification.

Voice and style

Authors use voice and style to show what their individual viewpoint is about the subject. For instance the author may choose to use a voice that is humorous and a style of writing that will make a reader laugh. This shows that the author thinks the subject of the article is not very serious. An author may choose to use a persuasive voice and a style that will persuade the reader of a point of view. This shows how the author feels about this particular topic, that the author either argues for it or is against it. An author may choose to use a very analytical style of writing. This shows that the author thinks the subject is worthy of study. There are many different voices and styles of writing. When reading an article, the reader should be aware of the author's voice and style.

Example
Identify the voice in the passage below.
When I was 12, every guy played stickball and all you needed was a broomstick and a rubber ball. We played for a couple of hours every day in the street, and when we weren't playing stickball, we played box ball and stoop ball. Kids today have never heard of these old games. Now they are more interested in computer games than sports.

To identify the voice of the passage, the reader needs to look for clues to see what the voice says and suggests. The reader needs to figure out who the voice is and what it feels about its topic. In this passage, the voice is talking about his past and the games that he used to play. The games seem old-fashioned and the voice even says that kids "today have never heard of these old games." The voice seems a bit nostalgic for the old days. The voice also suggests that today's kids are only interested in computer games. This suggests that the voice does not completely approve of computer games and that it is partial to sports.

Drafts

Coherence, progression, and logical support of ideas
Coherence is very important when writing because without it the reader will not be able to understand what is being written. If the reader has to ask "What does that mean?" then the writer did not succeed in getting the point across. When revising a draft, always look at the writing to be sure that it is clear and easy to understand. At the same time, there must be a beginning, middle, and an end. Ideas need to progress in a natural order so that the reader does not have to go back and reread sections to get the meaning. Also, the ideas need to have supporting details.

Revision
When revising a draft, make sure the writing is clear. Look over each paragraph carefully and check to see if something has to be added or taken out. Look to see if an idea has to be supported in more detail. See if rearranging the order of the paragraphs will help the writing make more sense. If a paragraph is too long, perhaps it needs to be cut into two paragraphs. Check for errors in spelling and punctuation as well. The writing should progress easily and naturally. Any ideas that are brought up should have enough support behind them. Reread the draft, make the changes that are needed, and make sure that the purpose of the writing is clear.

Revisions

There are many ways to revise writing. It is important to check for the logic of ideas and make sure the text has cohesion and belongs together. There must also be a progression of ideas that a reader can follow. The ideas should fit naturally with one another. After the writing is done, there are other ways to revise it. Sometimes sentences need to be rearranged or even deleted. Sometimes sentences need to be added to put more information into the text. Sometimes sentences need to be combined so that the sentences are more varied. The best way to revise a text is by rereading it carefully to see if the writing makes sense and flows well and then to make the appropriate changes.

Adding or deleting a sentence
A paragraph is a group of sentences that are about one main idea. All of the sentences should support the main idea of the paragraph and they should be arranged in an order that

makes sense. There should be a topic sentence that tells the main idea at the start of the paragraph. The other sentences should support the topic sentence. After writing a first draft, the writer should go back and read each paragraph carefully. If a sentence does not support the main idea, it should be deleted. Or, if the writer thinks that more information is needed to support the main idea, another sentence should be added.

Editing

Editing has many purposes. One important purpose is to make sure that standard English is being used. This means checking to see if the verb tenses are correct and if the verbs agree with their subject. This also means checking for other grammatical mistakes including the correct use of punctuation and spelling. Pronouns need to be checked so the correct form is used and pronoun antecedents or referents must be checked to see if they agree with each other. Another main purpose of editing is to ensure that there are varied sentences used and that the writing flows from one idea to another. Again, an editor would look for the appropriate word choices to make the writing more specific and engaging.

<u>Example 1</u>
Identify which sentence in the following passage should be deleted and tell why:

(1) In Japan, the drinking of tea is an elaborate ceremony. (2) Japanese tea is green. (3) The Japanese tea ceremony takes place on special occasions in a quiet room used for this purpose. (4) The room may be decorated with one of the elegant flower arrangements the Japanese are famous for. (5) Guests sit on cushions while the tea master prepares the tea. (6) Conversation is limited to the ritual taking place. (7) The tea ceremony is based on the Zen Buddhist belief that we should create beauty and serenity in the ordinary events of everyday life.
A 2, B 4, C 5, D 7

This passage is about the tradition of drinking tea in Japan. It tells where the tea ceremony takes place and how the room is decorated. It describes where the guests sit and how the conversation is limited to the ritual. It also tells why the tea ceremony is important to Zen Buddhist beliefs. There is only one sentence that does not fit into the context of the passage. This is choice A, sentence number 2. It says that Japanese tea is green, but the passage is not about the kind of tea that is used; it is about the ceremony, so it should be deleted.

<u>Example 2</u>
Identify which sentence is irrelevant to the passage below:
(1) Rear-end collisions are the second most common kind of car accident. (2) Over three million occur each year in the United States alone. (3) Experts say that one simple change to cars can help reduce the chances of a rear-end collision dramatically. (4) The goal is to make cars more visible so that drivers will see that a car is slowing down and put on the brake before it is too late. (5) My brother Randy drives a truck.

This paragraph is about rear-end collisions and how they are very common. That is the main idea. The first sentence is a topic sentence and tells the main idea. The other sentences should support the topic sentence. Sentence 2 supports the topic sentence, since it tells how many accidents of this kind occur a year in the United States. Sentence 3 gives more information about this kind of accident and how experts think they can reduce the number of them. Sentence 4 continues to give more information about the main idea. Sentence 5 is about the writer's brother and the fact that he drives a truck. It has nothing to do with the main idea and needs to be deleted.

Example 3

Identify which word could be substituted for the underlined word in the sentence below to make the sentence more precise.

Birds of paradise are usually colorful birds, although some are plain.

A. boring
B. uninteresting
C. dull
D. drab

Choice D is the best answer. This word is much more precise than *plain* is, and it gives the reader a better idea of just what the birds look like. Choice A, *boring,* isn't a good word to describe a bird. Both choice B and C are possible answers, but they are not as precise as the word *drab* is and wouldn't give as clear a picture of the birds that are not colorful.

Example 4

Choose the best word to substitute for the underlined word in the passage below and explain why it is the best choice.

Sheila had been standing by the bus stop for nearly a half-hour. It was raining hard now and she was getting wet. Her hair was dangling over her eyes and her coat was completely soaked. She tried to seek shelter under a canopy, but there was no room left.

A. drenched
B. damp
C. moist
D. sprayed

Sheila's hair "is dangling over her eyes" and her coat "is completely soaked." She is more than just wet so this word is inadequate. The best word to substitute for the word *wet* is choice A, *drenched.* She is really, really wet and this word is much more precise than *wet,* since it suggests she was soaked through. Choice B could not be substituted, since *damp* means only a little wet, and neither C nor D is a good choice either, since *moist* means a little wet also; there is no mention of her being *sprayed,* so that is incorrect as well.

Proofreading

Example 1

Proofread the following paragraph and tell what corrections should be made:

Pablo Picasso was one of the more gifted artists in history. Many of his drawings; and paintings are masterpieces. His work was found in museums' all around the world. Picasso will paint in many different styles, which have been copied by other artists. He hated war and tries to depict it's horrors in his paintings.

In the first sentence a comparative form of the adjective *gifted* is used instead of the superlative form, which would be correct. The word more should be replaced with the word *most.* In the second sentence, a semicolon is placed where none is needed. It should be deleted. In the third sentence the word *museums* is in a possessive form and that is incorrect. The apostrophe should be deleted. In the fourth sentence the verb *is* in the future tense, but it should be in the past tense; it should be *painted* not *will paint,* since the action took place in the past. In the last sentence there are two mistakes. The verb *tries* is in the present tense but should be *tried,* in the past tense. The word *it's* is incorrect. This word means *it is*, but what the context calls for is the possessive pronoun *its*.

Example 2

Proofread and correct the passage below:

> (1) More than two thousand years ago, there was a country that didn't like your neighbors. (2) It built the most longest fence in the world. (3) The country was China and the fence had been called the Great Wall of China. (4) It's surfaces are made of earth and stone and faced with brick. (5) It reaches 25 feet into the air and is very wide on top and their are watchtowers about 40 feet high that are placed at intervals of approximately every 200 yards.

There are several errors in the passage. In sentence 1, there is an incorrect choice of possessive pronoun. The pronoun *your* does not agree with its antecedent which is *China*. The correct possessive pronoun is *its*. In sentence 3 an incorrect form of the superlative adjective of *long* is used. The correct superlative form is *longest.* One syllable adjectives add the *–est* ending. They do not use the word *most* and *–est* adjectives and *most* are never used together. Sentence 3 has an incorrect form of the verb *call.* The correct form is *was called* instead of *had been called.* Sentence 4 uses the contraction form of *it is*, which is incorrect instead of the correct possessive pronoun *its.* Sentence 5 uses the wrong homonym; the word should be the adverb *there* rather than the possessive pronoun *their.*

Correct sentences

Example 1

Tell which sentence is written correctly and why it is correct:

A. Jeff went to the school's varsity team's ball game yesterday, yet he had a hot dog and a soda.
B. Jeff went to the school's varsity team's ball game yesterday, but he had a hot dog and a soda.
C. Jeff went to the school's varsity team's ball game yesterday and he had a hot dog and a soda.
D. Jeff went to the school's varsity team's ball game yesterday, or he had a hot dog and a soda.

The only sentence that is written correctly is choice C. The coordinating conjunction *and* is the correct choice. The two actions in the sentence are parallel. The coordinating conjunction *and* indicates that the two ideas are joined. Choice A is not correct, since the coordinating conjunction *yet* indicates an opposing relationship between the two parts of the sentence. This doesn't exist. Choice B is also incorrect. Again the coordinating conjunction *but* indicates an exception. But there is none here. Choice D is incorrect also, since the coordinating conjunction *or* indicates the possibility of a choice between two options. That doesn't exist here.

Example 2

Tell why the following sentence is not written correctly and how to correct it:

> Japanese karate masters' makes there hands and feet tough by striking it on padded surfaces or wood.

There are many errors in the sentence that need to be corrected. The word *masters'* is in a possessive form, but there is nothing that is owned by the masters so it is incorrect and should be written *masters* instead, a simple plural of the word master. The verb *makes* does not agree with the plural subject, *masters*. It should be changed to *make*. There should be a plural possessive pronoun in front of the word *hands*, but it is misspelled and should be *their*. The objective pronoun it in the prepositional phrase *by striking it* does not agree with its antecedent, the word, *hands*. This objective pronoun should be changed to the plural form, *them*.

Example 3

Tell which choice belongs in the empty space in the following sentence and explain why:

> The leather couch in the principal's office is the _______ one I've ever had the pleasure to sit on.

A. most best
B. better
C. goodest
D. best

Choice D is the correct answer. This is the superlative form of the adjective *good*. The sentence needs a superlative form because it is comparing the couch with more than one other couch. Choice A is not correct because it is a double superlative form—*most* and *best* are both superlative forms, but it is not correct to use two at the same time. Choice B is the comparative form of *good* and would be appropriate if the sentence were comparing two couches, but that is not the case. Choice C has the *–est* suffix, which many superlative adjectives take. But the word *goodest* does not exist, so it is incorrect also.

Example 4

Tell which sentence is written correctly and why it is correct. Explain why the other choices are incorrect and how to correct them.

A. When I was in the shower washing my hair, the phone rang.
B. We were eating the vegetables that will grow in our garden.
C. In a few minutes, we stops waiting to see if the mail is here.
D. The football team will practice this afternoon if it didn't rain.

Choice A is correct because the action takes place in the past so the verbs should both be in the past tense; the verbs also agree with the subject, since they are both singular. Choice B is incorrect, since it is clear that the action is in the past, but the second verb is in a future tense. The verb should be *grew* instead of *will grow*. Choice C is incorrect because the action is in the future, but the verb is in a present tense, and it is in a singular verb form not a plural form. The verb should be *will stop* not *stops*. Choice D is incorrect because the first part of the sentence shows that the action is in the future, but the second verb is in a past tense so the verb *didn't* should be *doesn't*.

Example 5
Identify the sentence that is not written correctly and tell how to correct it:

A. Ken was walking toward his bike, since he was going to ride it to the baseball game that he was pitching.
B. Marina thought about taking a picture of the lake with her new camera but decided to wait until the light was better.
C. A few weeks ago my friends and me were discussing whether to go out for the soccer team or not.
D. Many students were surprised when they received their grades on the math quiz because they did better than expected.

Choice C is not written correctly. The sentence calls for a subject pronoun not an object pronoun. The subject pronoun is *I*, so the sentence should read "A few weeks ago my friends and I were discussing whether to go out for the soccer team or not." The other sentences all use the correct form of pronoun. In choice A the pronouns *his* and *he* both refer to Ken so they are correct. In choice B, the pronoun *her* refers to Marina so it is correct. In choice D the pronouns *they* and *their* agree with the antecedent *students.*

Example 6
Identify the sentence that is not written correctly and tell how to correct it:

A. Bruce has done his homework and now he wants to shoot baskets.
B. Shannon put on her glasses and looked at the note closely.
C. Have the books we ordered been delivered to the library?
D. The dancers finished performing and then they go home.

Choice D is not correct because the verbs do not agree. The first verb is in the past tense, but the second verb is in the present tense; they need to both be in the past tense because the action has already taken place. The sentence should read: "The dancers finished performing and then they went home." Choice A is correct; in this case the first verb is in the past tense, because the action took place in the past, while the second verb is in the present tense, since the action is in the present tense. The action in choice B is in the past so both verbs need to be in the past tense and the same is true of choice D.

Variety of sentence types

It is important to use different types of sentences in order to add variety to the writing. A good writer uses simple sentences, compound sentences, and complex sentences. A simple sentence contains a subject and a verb and is a complete thought. A compound sentence has two independent ideas that are joined by a conjunction such as *for, and, but,* and *so*. A complex sentence is made up of an independent clause and at least one dependant clauses. A writer uses different types of sentences to make the writing more interesting to the reader and to keep the reader's attention. The use of different kinds of sentences also helps the writer create the style of writing that he or she wants.

Sentence fragment and run-on sentence

A sentence is a group of words that has a subject and a verb and contains a complete thought. A fragment is missing either the subject or the verb, which means it is not a complete thought. "All of the students" is not a complete thought because, while it has a subject, it does not have a verb. A fragment can be missing either the subject or the verb.

A run-on sentence has two complete thoughts that should be two separate sentences: "My class is going on a picnic it will be next week." This is a run-on sentence and it needs to be broken up into two sentences. "My class is going on a picnic. It will be next week." Run on sentences can also be corrected by placing a semi-colon between the two ideas: "My class is going on a picnic; it will be next week."

Example 1

Identify the sentence that is a sentence fragment in the passage below and explain how it could be corrected.

> (1) I looked in my backpack for my locker key but couldn't find it.(2) Searching the floor around my locker. (3) I still couldn't find it! (4) I emptied all my pockets, but still no luck. (5) Unfortunately, I had left it at home.

Sentence 1 has a subject and a verb, so it is a complete sentence not a fragment. Sentence 2 does not have a subject. It is a fragment. Sentence 3 has a subject and a verb and sentences 4 and 5 have both a subject and a verb too. In order to correct sentence 2, the writer needs to add a subject. Probably the easiest way to correct it is to join it together with sentence 3. The writer would need to put a comma after the word *locker* and then it would have a subject, *I,* and be a complete thought. In this way the fragment becomes a dependant clause.

Example 2

Identify the run-on sentence in the following passage and explain how to correct it.

> (1) Mosquitoes are dangerous creatures most people aren't aware of how harmful they can be. (2) Some mosquitoes carry a disease called encephalitis that can be fatal. (3) The tree-hole mosquito gives a painful bite that can be deadly. (4) Even ordinary mosquitoes can make a summer evening a miserable experience.

Sentence 1 is a run-on because it contains two separate ideas. Sentence 2 is not a run-on, nor are the other sentences in the passage. They all express one idea. There is more than one way to correct sentence 1. One way is to join the two sentences with the conjunction *but,* so that the sentence would read: "Mosquitoes are dangerous creatures but most people aren't aware of how harmful they can be." Another way to correct the run-on sentence is to place a semi-colon after the word *creatures,* so it would read: "Mosquitoes are dangerous creatures; most people aren't aware of how harmful they can be."

Transition words

Choose the transition word that most effectively links the ideas in the sentence below:

> The doctor performed an emergency operation; _____ he saved the man's life.

A. nevertheless
B. for example
C. consequently
D. however

Each of the transition words has a different meaning and needs to be used accordingly. There is a relationship between the two ideas in the sentence. The doctor performed an operation and as a result he saved the man's life. Choice A nevertheless does not suggest a result. It suggests just the opposite. For example in choice B does not suggest a result either.

Choice D, however does not suggest a result. The only choice that does is choice C, consequently. As a consequence of the doctor performing the surgery, the man was saved so choice C is the correct answer.

Supporting details

Identify which sentence could be added after sentence 3 to provide supporting detail:

> (1) Monarch butterflies make a yearly migration that is one of the wonders of nature. (2) Every fall the butterflies fly south from many different places to their winter homes in the Monterey Peninsula of California and in the mountains near Mexico City. (3) It is a sight of rare beauty to see thousands of monarchs at one time. (4) In the spring, the butterflies mate and fly north again. (5) Most of these butterflies die on the return trip north. (6) Somehow their offspring continue the journey to a home they have never seen. (7) Then, the next fall, these butterflies repeat the trip south.

A. Life is difficult and dangerous for these tiny creatures.
B. Monarchs have beautiful orange-and-black patterned wings.
C. Monarch and Viceroy butterflies look very much alike.
D. Birds avoid eating Monarchs because they taste bad.

Choice B is the correct answer because this sentence fits in best with the information in sentence 3 because it gives details about what the butterflies look like. Choice A doesn't relate to sentence 3. It talks about how difficult life is for the butterflies. It doesn't tell why they are beautiful to look at. Choice C gives information about the different kinds of butterflies, but it doesn't support sentence 3, so it is not the correct choice. Choice D has more information about Monarch butterflies, but it does not relate to sentence 3 so it is also incorrect.

Possessives

Possessive nouns show ownership. They often use apostrophes and the letter "s." For instance, a writer might say, "The house of the Owens is near a lake," but this is awkward so instead ownership is shown by using an apostrophe and the letter "s" to make the name "Owens" into a possessive. The writer would then say, "The Owens' house is near the lake." The apostrophe and "s" take the place of the "of" to show ownership or possession. The writer can check to see if a possessive is correct by inserting the word "of" instead of using the apostrophe and "s" and inverting the order of the words to see if the sentence makes sense.

Verb tenses

Verb tenses are ways in which verbs show that an action takes place. Verbs change according to when an action occurs. An action can take place in the present tense, which means the action is happening right now. An action can take place in the past tense, which means the action has already happened and is in the past. An action can take place in the future, which means the action has not yet happened but will do so. A progressive tense shows that the action is ongoing and continuing to go on in the present.

Compound sentence and complex sentence

A compound sentence differs from a simple sentence because it has two or more main clauses, with each main clause having its own subject and predicate. The clauses of compound sentences are usually joined by a comma and a coordinating conjunction, such as *and, but, or, nor, yet,* or *for.* An example of a compound sentence is: Harry plays soccer, but Jim plays the guitar. A complex sentence has one main clause and one or more subordinate clauses. Two main clauses may also be joined by a semicolon. An example of a complex sentence is: It is difficult to do homework when you are tired.

Pronoun referents

Pronoun referents or antecedents are the word or group of words that a pronoun refers to. All pronouns must agree with their antecedents in number, gender, and person. A pronoun antecedent may be a noun, another pronoun, or a phrase or clause acting as a noun. Read the following sentence. "Lawyers must research their cases thoroughly." In this example the pronoun referent or antecedent is the noun *lawyers.* The pronoun *their* refers to *lawyers.* It agrees with its antecedent because it is a plural pronoun. "Marian loved her new bicycle." In this sentence the pronoun *her* refers to *Marian.* It is correct because it agrees with the subject, since it is a singular feminine pronoun.

Prepositional phrase

A prepositional phrase is a group of words that begins with a preposition and ends with a noun or pronoun that is called the object of the preposition. "The van goes to the airport." In this sentence the prepositional phrase is *to the airport* with *to* being the preposition and *airport* the object. Prepositional phrases can have more than one object. "The van goes to the airport and the metro." In this sentence both *airport* and *metro* are objects of the preposition. Prepositional phrases can act as adjectives or adverbs. Adjectival prepositional phrases modify a noun or pronoun. An adverbial prepositional phrase modifies a verb, adjective, or an adverb.

Objective case pronoun

An objective pronoun is a pronoun that takes the place of a noun that is an object or indirect object of a verb and the object noun in a prepositional phrase. The objective pronouns are: *me, you, him, her, it, us,* and *them.* Some objective pronouns are masculine, feminine or neuter, such as *him, her,* and *it.* They are either singular or plural. In the sentence: "The ball was pitched and Bill hit it out of the stadium," *it* is the object of the verb *hit;* it is a singular neuter form, since it refers to *ball.* Objective pronouns are used as indirect objects as well. "Sally gave Mike and us a piece of pie." Here the indirect objects of the verb are *Mike* and *us.* Objective pronouns are used in prepositional phrases. "Vera put the blanket over her." In this case *her* is the object of the preposition *over.*

Pronoun

Identify which sentence uses pronouns correctly and explain why.

A. The best dancers in the school are her and me.
B. He and I are going to the concert next week.
C. She and me had fun swimming at the beach.
D. The coach picked Luis and I to be on the team.

Choice B is the correct answer. This is the only sentence that uses pronouns correctly. This sentence calls for pronouns that are subjects and both *he* and *I* are the subject form of these pronouns. Choice A is not correct because subject nouns should follow forms of the verb *to be*. The verb *are* cannot take an object and *her* and *me* are object forms of pronouns. Choice C is incorrect because the sentence requires subject pronouns. While *she* is a subject form, *me* is not. It should be changed to *I*. Choice D is incorrect because the verb *picked* takes object pronouns. *I* is a subject pronoun. This should be changed to *me*.

Conjunctions

Sentences can be joined together by using conjunctions like *and, but, yet,* and *or.* Each conjunction has a different meaning and should be chosen according to the context of the ideas. If two ideas are alike, they should be joined together with *and.* "Rona went to library. She studied for a history test." These ideas are alike. "Rona went to the library and she studied for a history test." If the ideas are different, use *but* or *yet.* "The food was cooking. It was nearly done." "The food was cooking, but it was nearly done." If there is a choice between ideas, use *or.* "You can come with me to the mall. You can stay at home." These ideas offer a choice. "You can come with me to the mall or you can stay at home."

Prepositional phrases

Prepositional phrases are made up of a preposition and an object. They can elaborate written ideas by giving more information about or modifying a noun or pronoun; these are called adjectival phrases. They can also give more information about or modify a verb, an adjective or an adverb; these are called adverbial phrases. They help to vary the writing and make it more precise. "The bus goes to the city on the island in the bay." In this sentence there are three prepositional phrases that modify the noun *city.* They help the reader learn more about where the city is located.

Combining sentences

Identify the best way to combine the sentences below without changing their meaning and explain why it is the best way:

Brad was practicing gymnastics. He twisted his ankle badly.

A. Brad was practicing gymnastics, he twisted his ankle badly.
B. Brad was practicing gymnastics; therefore he twisted his ankle badly.
C. Whenever Brad was practicing gymnastics, he twisted his ankle badly.
D. While Brad was practicing gymnastics, he twisted his ankle badly.

Choice D is the best answer because it uses the conjunction *while* to show how the events in the sentence are related. This suggests correctly that Brad twisted his ankle during the time he was practicing gymnastics. Choice A is incorrect because two sentences cannot be joined by a comma alone. This mistake is called a comma splice. Choice B is incorrect because it changes the meaning of the sentences and makes it sound as though practicing gymnastics always results in an ankle being twisted. Choice C is incorrect because it suggests that whenever Brad is at the gym he twists his ankle.

Revising sentences

Example 1

Describe how to rewrite the sentences below so they will read better:

I finished high school. I was given a gold pocket watch. My grandfather once owned it.

These sentences are all short and are all about the same topic. They can be put together to make a more complex and interesting sentence that will contain the same information, but make reading it a more complete experience. Here is one way a writer could change the sentences to improve the expression of the sentence.

After I finished high school, I was given a gold pocket watch that my grandfather once owned.

This revised sentence makes use of the conjunctive clause "When I finished high school" and the subjective clause "that my grandfather once owned" to make the sentence longer, more complex, and more interesting to read.

Example 2

Discuss what an editor could do to improve the awkwardness of the sentence below.

Shout for joy was what Renee did after the track meet she won.

The problem with the sentence is that the writer arranged the words in such a way that it is almost impossible to understand what was meant. The meaning of the sentence is not expressed well at all. It needs to be rearranged and reordered so that the reader can understand what is being said. An editor could improve the sentence by putting the action in the order in which it happened. For instance the order of this action is that Renee won the track meet and then she shouted for joy. Actually there are many ways that this sentence could be rewritten. "Renee shouted for joy after she won the track meet." This is one way. Another way is: "After she won the track meet, Renee shouted for joy." Now the meaning of the sentence is clear.

Comparative and superlative adjectives

A writer compares two nouns or pronouns by using a comparative adjective. There are two ways to form a comparative adjective: by adding an *–er* to the adjective or by putting the word *more* in front of the adjective. For instance the comparative form of the adjective "young" is "young*er*." The word *than* is usually used with a comparative adjective. "She is younger than I am." For adjectives that have three or more syllables, the word *more* is put in front of the adjective, for instance "more interesting."

The superlative form of adjectives is used when comparing three or more nouns or pronouns. The superlative form can be formed by adding *-est* to the adjective: "youngest." When the adjective has three or more syllables, the word *most* is inserted before the adjective: "the most interesting." Before all superlative forms the article *the* is inserted.

Subject-verb agreement

Identify the sentence with a verb that does not agree with the subject.

A. Nothing makes me as mad as cruelty to animals.

B. Everybody needs someone to care about.
C. Each of the lions was roaring loudly.
D. Only one of the players were chosen to be on the all-star team.

If there is a plural subject, the verb must be in a plural form; if the subject is singular, it needs to have a singular verb. Choice A is correct because the word *nothing* is singular and takes a singular verb. Choice B is also correct since the word *everybody* takes a singular verb. Choice C is correct too; the word *each* is considered singular and takes a singular verb. Choice D is the sentence where the verb does not agree with the subject. In this sentence the subject is *one* and it is singular. The verb *were*, however, is a plural form. This kind of mistake occurs often because a writer may confuse *players* for the subject. Another reason this mistake occurs is that the word *players* is right before the verb and *players were* sounds correct even though it is not.

Double negative

A double negative is when a writer uses two "no" type words in one sentence. In English, double negatives are incorrect. Negative words include *no, none, nothing, no one, nobody,* and *never.* Negative verbs use the word *not.* The rule is that if you use a negative word in a sentence, you cannot use a negative verb too. "She does not know no one" is incorrect. It can be corrected in two ways, since there are two negatives. "She does not know anyone" or "She knows no one" are both correct. The same is true of verb contractions—for example, *won't* is a contraction for *will not.* "Bill won't do nothing until the rain stops." This sentence has a double negative: *won't* and *nothing*. It needs to be corrected. "Bill won't do anything until the rain stops" or" Bill will do nothing until the rain stops" are correct.

Conventions of written language

The conventions of written language include using capitalization and punctuation correctly. Proper names, the first word of sentences, and titles should be capitalized. The names of countries, rivers, and states are all capitalized as well. Proper punctuation includes correct use of end marks, commas, semicolons, colons, and apostrophes. The conventions of written language also include making sure each sentence is complete. There should not be run-on or sentence fragments. Good penmanship is important, since it allows the reader to understand what has been written. The handwriting should be neat. Spelling is another important part of conventions. Words should be spelled correctly. To do this, it may be necessary to use a dictionary. By using these conventions, an author will be able to communicate more clearly.

Capitalization

Identify which sentence has incorrect capitalization and explain why:
A. Have you ever seen the movie *From Here to Eternity*?
B. Labor Day marks the end of summer for most people.
C. The Spanish Language is spoken throughout South America.
D. The exploration of the west was encouraged by President Thomas Jefferson.

Proper nouns; the names of cities, states, and countries; and the first word in a sentence should all be capitalized. There is one sentence that doesn't follow the rules of capitalization. Choice C is the sentence that does not have correct capitalization. While the word *Spanish* refers to a country and should be capitalized, the word *language* does not need to be capitalized. It is not a proper name. It does not refer to a country. Choice A uses the correct capitalization of the name of a movie. Choice B correctly capitalized Labor Day which is a holiday and Choice D is correct because it capitalizes president, since it is a title and the president's name.

Colon and semicolon

A colon may be used to introduce a list, especially after words such as *these, the following*, or *as follows*. Colons are used to introduce material that illustrates or explains the material that precedes it. They are used to introduce a long quotation. Colons are also used to separate the hour and minute in writing the time and after the salutation of a business letter. Semicolons are used to separate main clauses that are not joined by a coordinating conjunction or a conjunctive adverb. They are used to separate items in a series if those items contain commas, and they are used to separate two main clauses joined by a coordinating conjunction when the clauses have several commas.

Homonyms

A homonym is a word that sounds the same as another word but has a different meaning. It may also have a different spelling. For example, *wear* and *where* are homonyms. "Where is the concert?" In this sentence the meaning of *where* is "what place." "Wear your new outfit." In this sentence, *wear* means "to put on." You need to figure out which meaning is meant from the context of the sentence. Sometimes there are multiple homonyms. *There, their*, and *they're are* all homonyms. They all mean different things. Other homonyms include: *wait* and *weight*; *foreword* and *forward*; *pedal* and *peddle*; *principal* and *principle*; and *stationary* and *stationery*.

Writing Practice Test

Practice Questions

Questions 1-8 pertain to the following passage:

An American Hero

(1) In the year 1912, the unsinkable Titanic sank, the United States territory of Arizona became a state, and my Great Uncle Charlie was born. (2) Charlie was born in a small town in Kentucky. (3) On a farm. (4) He grew up learning about the seasons, when to plant the seeds, and when the crops were ripe for picking. (5) His mornings were spent with his hands in dirt as he tended to the growing corps.

(6) When Charlie was only 12, his father died. (7) He had to quit school to take care of his family. (8) While other children were learning and playing at school, Charlie worked in factories to help pay for his mother and sisters to eat. (9) Irregardless of how he felt about having to work, Charlie never complained.

(10) On December 7, 1941, Japan attacked the American naval base at Pearl Harbor. (11) Charlie enlisted in the army when he was 30 years old, and went to fight in the war. (12) He fought in six major battles, including landing in Normandy on D-Day. (13) While he was in the army, Charlie joined the United States horseshoe team and became the champion of the european allies. (14) After the war, Charlie returned to Kentucky married a woman named Bethany, and had three children.

(15) Today, Charlie can still be found with his hands in the dirt. (16) He loves to work in the small garden beside his front porch. (17) The bright colors of ripening strawberries, tomatoes, and ears of corn can be seen next to the house with Charlie walking though the rows of crops with his watering can. (18) He tends to them with love. (19) Charlie watches over his family like the crops in the garden, and that is why he is my hero.

1. What is the BEST way to explain the information in sentences 2 and 3?

Ⓐ Charlie was born in a small town in Kentucky. It was on a farm

Ⓑ Charlie was born in Kentucky. In a small town and on a farm

Ⓒ Charlie was born in a small town. In Kentucky, it was on a farm

Ⓓ Charlie was born in a small Kentucky town on a farm

2. What change, if any, should be made to sentence 5?

Ⓐ Change *corps* to *crops*

Ⓑ Change *were* to *was*

Ⓒ Insert a comma after *dirt*

Ⓓ Make no change

3. What change, if any, should be made to sentence 9?

Ⓐ Change *complained* to *complains*

Ⓑ Change *irregardless* to *regardless*

Ⓒ Delete the comma after *work*

Ⓓ Make no change

4. What sentence could BEST follow and support sentence 10?

Ⓐ Pearl Harbor is a naval base in Hawaii

Ⓑ The USS Arizona was one of the battleships that sank

Ⓒ This event directly led into the United States' involvement in World War II

Ⓓ Charlie had never been to Hawaii

5. What change, if any, should be made to sentence 13?

Ⓐ Change *european* to *European*

Ⓑ Change *became* to *becomes*

Ⓒ Insert a comma after *champion*

Ⓓ Make no change

6. What change, if any, should be made to sentence 14?

Ⓐ Change *returned* to *returns*

Ⓑ Insert a comma after *Kentucky*

Ⓒ Insert *and* after *Kentucky*

Ⓓ Make no change

7. What change, if any, should be made in sentence 16?

Ⓐ Change *loves* to *loved*

Ⓑ Insert a comma after *garden*

Ⓒ Change *beside* to *besides*

Ⓓ Make no change

8. What change, if any, should be made in sentence 17?

Ⓐ Change *colors* to *colours*

Ⓑ Delete the comma after *strawberries*

Ⓒ Change *though* to *through*

Ⓓ Make no change

Questions 9 – 16 pertain to the following story:

The Top Deck

(1) We walked outside through the sliding glass doors and waited in line for the large, double-decker red bus. (2) My family flew to London for a week in July to celebrate my sisters graduation. (3) She wore a blue cap and gown. (4) The sky was gray, and light puddles spotted the ground. (5) As the bus pulled up against the curb, dirty water splashed our feet.

(6) The driver's seat was on the opposite side of the bus, and the driver smiled at me when I showed him my ticket. (7) I looked out the window and realised that we were driving on the opposite side of the street. (8) All around us people who were on the wrong side of the street driving from what looked like the passenger seat. (9) The bus was filled with people. (10) Almost every seat was taken, and people were even standing in the aisle holding onto handrails and poles. (11) Their was a spiral staircase directly behind the driver, and we walked up it to try and find more seats. (12) There were two rows of seats upstairs and a large window that looked onto the streets. (13) For seats were open near the front of the bus and we hurried to get them.

(14) The bus stopped every few seconds, and each time I had to hold onto my seat to keep from sliding into the aisle. (15) "What street are we looking for?" my dad asked my mom. (16) "Oxford" she replied. (17) I looked out the giant window. (18) We passed a large building that was shaped like an egg, and we continued to travel. (19) The bus driver's voice came over the speakers. (20) "Now approaching Liverpool," he said

(21) My mom looked at my dad. (22) I grabbed my sister's arm, but she was busy taking pictures of the buildings out the window. (23) "Liverpool," my mom whispered with a worried look on her face. (24) "We're lost, aren't we?" my dad said.

9. What change, if any, should be made in sentence 2?

Ⓐ Change *flew* to *flied*

Ⓑ Change *week* to *weak*

Ⓒ Change *sisters* to *sister's*

Ⓓ Make no change

10. What change, if any, should be made in sentence 7?

Ⓐ Change *realised* to *realize*

Ⓑ Change *street* to *streat*

Ⓒ Change *looked* to *look*

Ⓓ Make no change

11. What change, if any, should be made in sentence 11?

Ⓐ Delete the comma after *driver*

Ⓑ Change *Their* to *There*

Ⓒ Change *staircase* to *stair case*

Ⓓ Make no change

12. What change should be made in sentence 13?

Ⓐ Change *open* to *opened*

Ⓑ Change *were* to *was*

Ⓒ Change *For* to *Four*

Ⓓ Change *hurried* to *hurried*

13. Which of the following is the BEST way to rewrite the ideas in sentence 8?

Ⓐ All around us people were driving from what looked like the passenger seat, and they were driving on the opposite side of the street

Ⓑ All around us people who were on the wrong side of the street, driving from what looked like the passenger seat

Ⓒ All around us people were driving on the wrong side of the street. Driving from what looked like the passenger seat

Ⓓ All around us people were driving from what looked like passenger seat, they were on the opposite side of the street

14. What change, if any, should be made in sentence 16?

Ⓐ Change *Oxford* to *oxford*

Ⓑ Insert a comma after *Oxford*

Ⓒ Insert a period after the quotation mark

Ⓓ Make no change

15. Which sentence does not belong in this essay?

Ⓐ Sentence 20

Ⓑ Sentence 6

Ⓒ Sentence 13

Ⓓ Sentence 3

16. What is the BEST transition word or phrase that could be added to the beginning of sentence 19?

Ⓐ However

Ⓑ Once in a while

Ⓒ Additionally

Ⓓ After a while

Questions 17 -24 pertain to the following story:

Longhorn Café

(1) Last Saturday night my dad took me to watch the Longhorns play football in Austin. (2) It was a cool evening, and the orange-painted stadium was filled with screaming fans. (3) Even though we live in San Antonio, my dad has always been a dedicated Longhorns fan, and he wears his orange proudly.

(4) We arrived in Austin early. (5) "Traffic," my dad said as his only explanation. (6) He parked the truck down a small side street and motions for me to get out and follow him. (7) "I want to take you someplace," he said. (8) "I used to come here all the time when I was in college. (9) We walked up to a small building with a large patio off to the side. (10) A large tree with low branches spread across the patio and connected with the roof. (11) The leaves were beginning to change colors, and it was like sitting under a leafy canopy.

(12) We sat at a table outside on a rusting rocking bench beside an abandoned bathtub. (13) Stands of colored lights hung across the patio. (14) Wrapped around the tree. (15) "What is this place?" I asked. (16) My dad

smiled and pointed to a sign bordered with colored lights. (17) "Spider Café," he said. (18) All around us, people were drinking coffee and staring at them computer screens. (19) Our waiter was named Chris, and he had a long beard, wore a dirtied apron, and carried empty coffee mugs.

(20) The waited came up to us, and my dad ordered himself a latte and a sweet drink for me. (21) My dad looked around the patio and smiled. (22) He leaned into the bench and placed his hand on the side of the bathtub. (23) He didn't even mind when he spilled coffee onto his favorite orange shirt. (24) "You'll love it here," he said, "when you are a Longhorn football player?"

17. What change, if any, should be made in sentence 5?

Ⓐ Delete the comma after *traffic*

Ⓑ Insert a comma after *said*

Ⓒ Change *said* to *says*

Ⓓ Make no change

18. What change should be made in sentence 6?

Ⓐ Change *parked* to *park*

Ⓑ Change *street* to *Street*

Ⓒ Insert a comma after *street*

Ⓓ Change *motions* to *motioned*

19. What change, if any, should be made in sentence 8?

Ⓐ Change *come* to *came*

Ⓑ Change *to* to *too*

Ⓒ Insert a quotation mark after *college*

Ⓓ Make no change

20. What revision, if any, is needed in sentences 13 and 14?

Ⓐ Strands of colored lights hung across the patio wrapped, around the tree

Ⓑ Strands of colored lights hung across the patio and wrapped around the tree

Ⓒ Strands of colored lights hung. Across the patio, wrapped around the tree

Ⓓ No revision is needed

21. **What change, if any, should be made in sentence 18?**

● Change *them* to *their*

Ⓑ Delete the comma after *us*

Ⓒ Insert a comma after *and*

Ⓓ Make no change

22. **Where is the best placement for sentence 19?**

Ⓐ After sentence 22

● After sentence 20

Ⓒ Before sentence 18

Ⓓ No change is needed

23. **What change, if any, should be made in sentence 20?**

Ⓐ Change *ordered* to *orders*

Ⓑ Change *himself* to *hisself*

● Change *waited* to *waiter*

Ⓓ Make no change

24. **What change should be made in sentence 24?**

Ⓐ Change *Longhorn* to *longhorn*

Ⓑ Change *you are* to *your*

Ⓒ Change *football* to *Football*

● Change the question mark to a period

Questions 25 – 32 pertain to the following story:

Strike Three

(1) As I stared down at the hitter in the batters box, I remembered what my dad had said to me. (2) "Shut everything out." (3) I focused on the glove in front of me. (4) I looked into the deep, blackened pocket, and sawed my target. (5) The batter tapped his bat against the sides of his cleats, and rested the bat on his shoulders. (6) With hard eyes, he stares back at me.

(7) I kicked the front of my cleat into the bright white rubber on the pitching mound and took a deep breath. (8) Shut everything out," he had said. (9) Slowly the noises disappeared. (10) I could no longer hear the shouts from the parents in the stands. (11) In my head, I silenced the cheers from both

dugouts. (12) The umpire did not exist. (13) There were no players, no coaches, not even a catcher. (14) There was just me. (15) The ball and the glove.

(16) I took a deep breath and brought my hands together at my chest. (17) I looked over at first base, but there was no runner. (18) In one motion, my feet left the rubber and connected with ground. (19) Dirt flew in the air as my arm rotated forward and released the ball in front of me. (20) I watched as the ball spun and landed into glove with a hard crack. (21) The umpire shot up from his crouched position and pointed his finger to the right and yelled, "Strike Three!"

(22) The noises came back. (23) The crowd cheered in the stands and I could here stomping feet. (24) My teammate clapped his hand to its glove and ran toward me. (25) My coach raised a first into the air in celebration. (26) I was surrounded by my teammates, and they were patting me on the back. (27) My dad was sitting on a bleacher behind home plate. (28) He raised his thumb to me and smiled as I ran off the field with my teammates.

25. What change, if any, should be made in sentence 1?

Ⓐ Change *stared* to *starred*

Ⓑ Change *dad* to *Dad*

Ⓒ Change *batters* to *batter's*

Ⓓ Make no change

26. What change should be made in sentence 4?

Ⓐ Change *blackened* to *blacked*

Ⓑ Change *sawed* to *saw*

Ⓒ Delete the comma after *deep*

Ⓓ Change *into* to *in to*

27. What change, if any, should be made in sentence 6?

Ⓐ Change *stares* to *stared.*

Ⓑ Change *me* to *I*

Ⓒ Delete the comma after *eyes*

Ⓓ Make no change

28. What change should be made in sentence 8?

Ⓐ Change *everything* to *every thing*

Ⓑ Delete the comma after *out*

Ⓒ Change the comma after *out* to a period

Ⓓ Insert quotation marks before *Shut*

29. What is the best way to combine sentence 14 and sentence 15?

Ⓐ There was just the ball, the glove, and me

Ⓑ There was just me, the ball, and the glove

Ⓒ There was just me and the ball and the glove

Ⓓ Make no change

30. What change, if any, should be made in sentence 23?

Ⓐ Change *cheered* to *cheer*

Ⓑ Change *here* to *hear*

Ⓒ Change *could* to *can*

Ⓓ Make no change

31. What sentence could BEST follow and support sentence 22?

Ⓐ My foot was still planted hard into the ground

Ⓑ The sounds came flooding into my ears as I looked up

Ⓒ I felt good

Ⓓ The umpire took off his mask and started walking toward the fence

32. What is the BEST transition word that could be added to the beginning of sentence 26?

Ⓐ However

Ⓑ Consequentially

Ⓒ Soon

Ⓓ Therefore

Questions 33 – 40 pertain to the following passage:

Imagine a Better World

(1) My favorite song is "imagine" by John Lennon. (2) It was released in 1971. (3) It is one of the few famous songs that John Lennon recorded and sang alone. (4) For the majority of his career, John Lennon was a member of an iconic rock band called the Beatles, a band that changed the music industry. (5) The Beatles accepted a lot of success in their career, with popular songs such as "I Want to Hold Your Hand," "Come Together," "Let it Be," and "Here Comes the Sun." (6) After the band decided to separate, John Lennon became a solo artist as well as an promoter for peace.

(7) "Imagine" tells the story of Lennons dream of peace in the world. He asks the listener to imagine different situations. (8) He says to imagine that there are no countries, religions, or possessions. (9) He says, "I wonder if you can." (10) This line strikes me the most I try to imagine such a world. (11) When talking about no possessions, he continues and says, "No need for greed or hunger." (12) It is a great line. (13) Throughout the song, he says, "Imagine all the people." (14) And he gives examples. (15) At first he says, "living for today," and then moves on to say, "living life in peace," and finally, "sharing all the world."

(16) My favorite part of the song is the chorus. (17) Lennon says, "You may say I'm a dreamer, but I'm not the only one. (18) I hope someday you'll join us, and the world will be as one." (19) When I really listen to the words of this song, I realize that "Imagine" is so much more than something that sounds nicely. (20) Lennon is saying something very important and suggesting ways in which the world can live in peace. (21) Because of this song, I am a dreamer as well, and I join John Lennon in the fight for world peace.

33. What change, if any, should be made in sentence 1?

Ⓐ Change *favorite* to *favourite*

● Change *imagine* to *Imagine*

Ⓒ Insert a comma after *song*

Ⓓ Make no change

34. What is the BEST verb to replace *accepted* in sentence 5?

Ⓐ Lasted

Ⓑ Liked

● Had

Ⓓ Watched

35. What change should be made in sentence 6?

Ⓐ Change *separate* to *separated*

Ⓑ Insert a comma after *artist*

Ⓒ Change *solo* to *Solo*

● Change *an* to *a*

36. What change, if any, should be made in sentence 7?

● Change *Lennons* to *Lennon's*

Ⓑ Change *dream* to *dreamt*

Ⓒ Insert a comma after *peace*

Ⓓ Make no change

37. What is the BEST way to revise sentence 10?

● This line strikes me the most as I try to imagine such a world.

Ⓑ This line strikes me the most, I try to imagine such a world.

Ⓒ This line strikes me, the most. I try to imagine such a world.

Ⓓ No revision needed.

38. What is the BEST way to combine sentence 13 and sentence 14?

Ⓐ Throughout the song, he says "Imagine all the people" and he gives examples.

● Throughout the song, he says, "Imagine all the people," and he gives examples.

Ⓒ Throughout the song he says Imagine all the people, and he gives examples.

Ⓓ Throughout the song he says Imagine all the people and he gives examples.

39. What change, if any, should be made in sentence 18?

● Insert a quotation mark before *I*

Ⓑ Move the period after the quotation marks

Ⓒ Change *you'll* to *youl'l*

Ⓓ Make no change

40. What change should be made in sentence 19?

Ⓐ Delete the comma after *song*

Ⓑ Change *something* to *some thing*

● Change *nicely* to *nice*

Ⓓ Change *realize* to *realized*

Answers and Explanations

TEKS Standard §110.19(b)(19)(C)

1. D: because this sentence is the simplest way to explain where Charlie was born. A is not correct because two sentences are not necessary. The additional subject and verb are unnecessary to express the idea. B is not correct, because *In a small town and on a farm* is a fragment. C is not correct, because the sentences contain awkward wording. The sentences need to be combined in order to express the idea in the simplest form.

TEKS Standard §110.19(b)(14)(D) and (21)

2. A: because in this sentence, *crops* has been misspelled as *corps*. B is not correct, because the subject of the sentence, *mornings*, is plural. Therefore, the verb also must be plural for correct subject verb agreement. C is not correct, because this sentence does not need a comma.

TEKS Standard §110.19(b)(21)

3. B: because irregardless is not a word. The correct word is *regardless.* A is not correct because *complains* is in the present tense, while the rest of the paragraph is in the past tense. C is not correct, because a comma is needed after an introductory clause.

TEKS Standard §110.19(b)(19)(A)(viii)

4. C: because this sentence supports both sentence 10 and sentence 11. The sentence supports the cause and effect idea that the attack on Pearl Harbor prompted the United States to become involved in the war, which caused Charlie to enlist in the army. A is not correct. Although this sentence provides new information, it does not link and support sentences 10 and 11. B is not correct. Although this sentence provides new information, it does not link and support sentences 10 and 11. D is not correct. Although this sentence provides new information, it does not link and support sentences 10 and 11.

TEKS Standard §110.19(b)(14)(D) and (20)(A)

5. A: because *European* is a proper noun and must be capitalized. B is not correct, because *becomes* is in the present tense, and the rest of the paragraph is written in the past tense. C is not correct, because a comma is not needed after *champion.*

TEKS Standard §110.19(b)(20)(B)(i)

6. B: because this sentence uses commas in a series as it lists aspects of Charlie's life after the war. Both *returned to Kentucky* and *married a woman named Bethany* are events that have happened and therefore need to be separated by a comma. A is not correct. *Returns* is in the present tense, and the rest of the paragraph is written in the past tense. C is not correct. The correct sentence uses commas in a series, and therefore only uses one *and* in the sentence.

TEKS Standard §110.19(b)(19)

7. D: because the sentence is correct as written. A is not correct. Although the rest of the essay is written in the past tense, the last paragraph begins with *Today* and is written in the present tense. Therefore, *loves* is correct. B is not correct, because this sentence does not need a comma. C is not correct. Both *beside* and *besides* are prepositions, but *beside* means

"next to" and *besides* means "in addition to" or "other than." *Beside* is used in this sentence as "next to."

TEKS Standard §110.19(b)(14)(D) and (21)

8. C: because in this sentence, *through* has been misspelled as *though*. A is not correct, because *colors* is spelled correctly. B is not correct, because this sentence needs a comma after *strawberries,* since the sentence contains a list and uses commas in a series.

TEKS Standard §110.19(b)(14)(D) and (20)(B)

9. C: In this sentence, *Sister's* is possessive and requires an apostrophe. A is not correct. *Flew* is the correct past tense of *fly*. B is not correct, because *week* is a noun and is spelled correctly.

TEKS Standard §110.19(b)(14)(D) and (21)

10. A: because *realized* is misspelled in this sentence. B is not correct, because *street* is spelled correctly. C is not correct, because *look* is in the present tense, while the essay is written in past tense.

TEKS Standard §110.19(b)(14)(D) and (21)

11. B: because a homonym has been misused. *There* is used to indicate a physical or abstract place, while *their* is used to indicate possession. A is not correct, because this sentence has two independent clauses joined by the conjunction *and*, and a comma is used before the conjunction. C is not correct, because *staircase* is one word.

TEKS Standard §110.19(b)(14)(D) and (21)

12. C: because a homonym has been misused. *Four* is a number. A is not correct, because in this sentence *open* is used as a noun rather than a verb and does not need to be in the past tense. B is not correct. *Were* is plural, and *was* is singular. The subject of the sentence, *seats*, is plural; therefore, the verb also must be plural for correct subject verb agreement. D is not correct, because *hurried* is spelled correctly.

TEKS Standard §110.19(b)(19)(B)

13. A: because this rewording of this sentence makes the meaning clear and is grammatically correct. B is not correct because this sentence is a fragment. C is not correct because the second sentence is a fragment. D is not correct because this sentence is a run-on sentence.

TEKS Standard §110.19(b)(14)(D) and (20)(B)

14. B: because a comma is needed before the closing quotation when the sentence is not completed with the quotation. A is not correct because *Oxford* is a proper noun and must be capitalized. C is not correct. The sentence does not end with the quotation; therefore, a comma, rather than a period, goes before the quotation mark.

TEKS Standard §110.19(b)(14)(B)

15. D: because this sentence this sentence provides new information that is not important to the rest of the essay. Answers A, B, and C are incorrect, because all of these sentences present content that is important to the essay.

TEKS Standard §110.19(b)(19)(A)(viii)

16. D: In the previous sentence, the phrase *we continued to travel*, suggests a passage of time. A proper transition into the next sentence would involve the acknowledgement that time has passed. A is not correct because *however* is not a good transition into the sentence. B is not correct. Although *once in a while* relates to time, it does not transition well into the sentence given the context of the previous sentence. C is not correct. *Additionally* is not a good transition into the sentence because it does not indicate a passage of time.

TEKS Standard §110.19(b)(19) and (20)

17. D: because the sentence is correct as written. A is not correct, because a comma is needed before the closing quotation when the sentence is not completed with the quotation. B is not correct because this sentence does not need a comma. C is not correct because *says* is in the present tense, and the essay is written in the past tense.

TEKS Standard §110.19(b)(19)(C)

18. D: because *motions* is in the present tense, and the rest of the essay is written in the past tense. B is not correct because *street* is not used in this sentence as a proper noun and does not need to be capitalized. C is not correct. A comma is unnecessary because the second sentence is not an independent clause.

TEKS Standard §110.19(b)(20)(B)

19. C: because a quotation mark is needed to end dialogue. A is incorrect because *come* is in the present tense, and the essay is written in the past tense. B is not correct. *Too* means "also" or an indication of excess.

TEKS Standard §110.19(b)(19)(C)

20. B: because this sentence is grammatically correct as written. A is not correct. The comma is misplaced and disrupts the sentence. C is not correct because the second sentence is a fragment. D is not correct because sentence 14 is a fragment.

TEKS Standard §110.19(b)(19)

21. A: because *their* indicates possession; *them* does not. *Computer screens* belong to the subject, *people*. B is not correct. *All around us* is an introductory clause and needs a comma. C is not correct. *Staring at them computer screens* is not an independent clause and therefore does not need a comma.

TEKS Standard §110.19(b)(14)(B)

22. B: because the sentence provides additional information about the waiter. The sentence should be placed after the waiter has been introduced in sentence 20. A is not correct. The subject of the paragraph has shifted to the father at sentence 21, and therefore a sentence involving information about the waiter would be out of place after sentence 22. C is not correct. Sentence 18 provides setting information. A sentence involving information about the waiter before this sentence would be out of place. D is not correct. This sentence provides additional information about the waiter and should not conclude a paragraph.

TEKS Standard §110.19(b)(14)(D) and (21)

23. C: because *waiter* has been misspelled. A is not correct. *Orders* is in the present tense, and the essay is written in the past tense. B is not correct because *himself* is the correct word, while *hisself* is not a word.

TEKS Standard §110.19(b)(14)(D) and (20)

24. D: because the sentence is a statement, not a question. Therefore, the sentence needs to be punctuated with a period. A is not correct. In this sentence, *longhorn* refers to the mascot of a sports team and is a proper noun. Proper nouns need to be capitalized. B is not correct. *You* and *are* in this sentence are used as both a subject and a verb. *Your* indicates possession. C is not correct. *Football* is not a proper noun and does not require capitalization.

TEKS Standard §110.19(b)(14)(D) and (20)

25. C: In this sentence, *batter's* is possessive and needs an apostrophe. A is not correct because *stared*, the past tense of the verb, *stare*, is spelled correctly. B is not correct. In this sentence, *dad* is not a proper noun, since it is not used as a name. *My* before *dad* indicates that it is not a proper noun.

TEKS Standard §110.19(b)(19)(A)(i)

26. B: because *saw* is the correct past tense of the verb, *see*. A is not correct because *blackened* is the correct adjective. C is not correct. A comma is needed to separate adjectives when each adjective separately describes the noun. D is not correct. *Into* is spelled correctly.

TEKS Standard §110.19(b)(19)(A)(i) and (C)

27. A: because *stares* is in the present tense, and the rest of the essay is in the past tense. *Stared* is the correct past tense of *stare*. B is not correct. *Me* is the object of the sentence because it is the recipient of the action, *stares*. I is traditionally used as a subject. C is not correct. *With hard eyes* is an introductory clause, and a comma is needed after the clause.

TEKS Standard §110.19(b)(14)(D) and (20)

28. D: It is correct because the quotation marks after *out* indicate dialogue. Quotation marks are needed before *Shut* to begin the dialogue. A is not correct. When used as a noun, *everything* is one word. B is not correct. A comma is needed before the closing quotation when the sentence is not completed with the quotation. C is not correct. The sentence is not completed with the quotation, and therefore it needs a comma rather than a period before the closing quotation.

TEKS Standard §110.19(b)(19)(C)

29. A: because this sentence is grammatically correct. B is not correct. When using the pronoun, *me*, in a series, it is always placed at the end of the series. C is not correct. The repetition of *and* is not grammatically correct. The nouns need to be separated using commas in a series.

TEKS Standard §110.19(b)(14)(D) and (21)

30. B: It is correct because a homonym has been misused. *Hear* indicates the act of hearing and listening. *Here* indicates location. A is not correct. *Cheer* is in the present tense, and the rest of the essay is in the past tense. C is not correct. *Can* is in the present tense, and the rest of the essay is in the past tense.

TEKS Standard §110.19(b)(19)(A)(viii)

31. B: It is correct because this sentence supports both sentence 22 and 23. The preceding sentence discusses noises coming back. The next logical sentence should have something to do with noises. A is not correct. Although this sentence provides new information, it does not link and support sentences 22 and 23. C is not correct. Although this sentence provides

new information, it does not link and support sentences 22 and 23. D is not correct. Although this sentence provides new information, it does not link and support sentences 22 and 23.

TEKS Standard §110.19(b)(19)(A)(viii)

32. C: because a proper transition into the next sentence would involve the acknowledgement that time has passed. A is not correct. *However* is not a good transition into this sentence since it does not require a shift in ideas. B is not correct. *Consequentially* is not a good transition into this sentence since it presents no cause and effect. D is not correct. *Therefore* is not a good transition into this sentence since it presents no cause and effect.

TEKS Standard §110.19(b)(20)(A)

33. B: because *imagine* is a proper noun. As the title of a song, it requires capitalization. A is not correct. *Favorite* is spelled correctly. C is not correct. *My favorite song* is not an introductory clause, so a comma is not needed.

TEKS Standard §110.19(b)(14)(C)

34. C: because the missing verb in this sentence must have something to do with possession, since it discusses the band's success. *Had* indicates possession. A, B, and D are incorrect, because these verbs do not fit within the sentence.

TEKS Standard §110.19(b)(14)(D)

35. D: It is correct because in the sentence, the article *an* is followed by a noun, *promoter*. *Promoter* begins with a consonant and a consonant sound and therefore must be followed by the article *a.* A is not correct. The verb in this sentence is *decided*, not *separate*, and therefore *separate* does not need to be in the past tense like the rest of the paragraph. B is not correct because the comma is unnecessary. C is not correct. *Solo* is not a proper noun and does not need to be capitalized.

TEKS Standard §110.19(b)(14)(D) and (20)

36. A: because *Lennon* is possessive in this sentence; therefore, it requires an apostrophe. B is not correct. In this sentence, *dream* is a noun rather than a verb, so it does not need to be in the past tense. C is not correct, because a comma is unnecessary.

TEKS Standard §110.19(b)(14)(D) and (19)

37. A: because the sentence is missing the article *as*. This is the simplest way to express the idea of the sentence. B is incorrect because this sentence is not grammatically correct. C is incorrect because the first sentence is grammatically incorrect.

TEKS Standard §110.19(b)(14)(D) and (20)(B)

38. B: because this is the simplest way to express the idea in a grammatically correct sentence. F is incorrect because a comma is missing after *song* and after *people*. H is incorrect because a comma is missing after *song*, and quotation marks are missing around the quotation, *"Imagine all the people."* J is not correct. A comma is missing after *song* and after *people*, and quotation marks are missing around the quotation, *"Imagine all the people."*

TEKS Standard §110.19(b)(14)(D)

39. D: It is correct because the sentence is correct. A is not correct. This sentence is part of a longer quotation that began in the previous sentence. Since the quotation is continuing, the sentence does not begin with quotation marks. B is not correct. In a quotation, the punctuation is placed before the ending quotation marks. C is not correct. *You'll* is the correct contraction of *you will*.

TEKS Standard §110.19(b)(19)(A)(iii)

40. C: because in this sentence *nice* is an adjective rather than an adverb. It describes the noun, *sounds*, not the verb. A is not correct. *When I really listen to the words of this song* is an introductory clause, and a comma is needed after the clause. B is not correct. *Something* is one word when used as a noun. D is not correct. Although most of the essay is in the past tense, the final paragraph is in the present tense. *Realized* is in the past tense.

Sample Composition

Write a composition about a time when you made a hard decision.

Last November, I was sitting in my third period math class when my teacher told me that she needed to talk to me after class. I was worried that I had done something wrong or had forgotten to turn in a homework assignment. I thought about it, but could not remember missing any assignments. I also thought that maybe I had failed the last test, but I felt that I had done well on it. When I finally talked to her, I was relieved to hear that she wanted to move me up into the accelerated math class. I immediately thought of my friend, Alex. He and I were in the same math class, and it was the only class we had together. I wanted to be in accelerated math, but I did not want to leave my friend.

When I came home from school, I told my parents what my teacher had said. "Wow!" my mom said, "That is great!" My dad smiled at me. "Good job," he said. "I am really proud of you." It made me happy to know that my parents were proud and excited for me. I was excited too, but I was also scared. I decided to talk to my mom about it. I told her that I did not want to leave class with Alex because we had no other classes together and that I was afraid. "What are you afraid of?" she asked. I told her that I was already behind in the accelerated math class, and that I was afraid I would not be able to catch up. I was also afraid that the class would be too hard for me.

"Well, that's a lot to think about," my mom said. She told me to look at everything I was afraid of and think about each thing. She said I needed a plan. She told me that if my teacher thought I could do well in the accelerated class, I should listen to her and believe in myself. I told her I thought that I could spend extra time with the new teacher learning the material that I had missed. "But what about Alex?" I said. I still did not want to leave my friend. "You always have recess," she said.

I decided to join the accelerated math class and am very happy. It was hard at first to keep up with the work that I had missed, but I like learning new things. I have made a lot of new friends, but I also see Alex at recess. We all have fun. The accelerated math class was better for me, and I am happy I made this hard decision.

Writing Practice Test

Practice Questions

Questions 1 – 8 pertain to the following story:

The Greek Festival

(1) Every October my family attends the Greek Festival at the Greek Orthodox Church close to our house. (2) We were first invited four years ago by one of my friends, Amelia. (3) Her family attends the Greek Orthodox Church and works several booths at the festival each year. (4) They telled us that everyone was welcome.

(5) When we first arrived at the festival, we could hear the music from the parking lot? (6) It was music that I had never heard before, and some of it was in another language. (7) Amelia told me later that it was traditional Greek music. (8) We also noticed the smells that seemed to come from all over the festival grounds. (9) All around us, there were signs for meat, pastry, coffee drinks, and other side dishes. (10) My mom's favorite were the grape leaves, and my dad loved the Baklava. (11) It is a dessert is made up baked thin sheets of pastry dough covered in a sweet sauce like honey. (12) Amelia suggested us eat it with ice cream and chocolate sauce. (13) As much as I liked the baklava, my favorite was the gyro pita. (14) Gyro is lamb meat in a warm pita with tomato, lettuce, onion, and a Greek sauce. (15) I ate two pitas and it was deliciously!

(16) After we had eaten, everyone gathered around the dance floor and watched as people from all different age groups danced traditional Greek dances. (17) The dancers were dressed in special clothing and black dress shoes.

(18) Amelia danced in the second group of dancers, and her mom tossed money toward her. (19) Soon, the dance floor was covered in dollar bills from all of the dancers families. (20) The food was great, the music was fun, and the dancing was even better. (21) We had a great time at the greek Festival, and now I look forward to it every year!

1. What change, if any, should be made in sentence 4?

Ⓐ Change everyone to every one

Ⓑ Change telled to told

Ⓒ Change welcome to welcomed

Ⓓ Make no change

2. What change should be made in sentence 5?

Ⓐ Change arrived to arrive

Ⓑ Change festival to Festival

Ⓒ Delete the comma after festival

Ⓓ Change the question mark to a period

3. What change, if any, should be made in sentence 10?

Ⓐ Change were to was

Ⓑ Change mom's to moms

Ⓒ Change loved to loves

Ⓓ Make no change

4. What revision, if any, is needed in sentence 11?

Ⓐ It is a dessert that is made up of baked thin sheets of pastry dough covered in a sweet sauce like honey.

Ⓑ It is a dessert, is made up baked thin sheets of pastry dough covered in a sweet sauce like honey.

Ⓒ It is a dessert. Made up baked thin sheets of pastry dough covered in a sweet sauce like honey.

Ⓓ No revision needed.

5. What is the BEST way to revise sentence 12?

Ⓐ Amelia suggested, us eat it with ice cream and chocolate sauce.

Ⓑ Amelia suggested to us eat it with ice cream and chocolate sauce.

Ⓒ Amelia suggested us eat it, with ice cream and chocolate sauce.

Ⓓ Amelia suggested that we eat it with ice cream and chocolate sauce.

6. What change, if any, should be made in sentence 15?

Ⓐ Change ate to eat

Ⓑ Change deliciously to delicious

Ⓒ Change two to too

Ⓓ Make no change

7. What change, if any, should be made in sentence 19?

Ⓐ Change covered to cover

Ⓑ Change from to form

● Change dancers to dancers'

Ⓓ Make no change

8. What change, if any, should be made in sentence 21?

Ⓐ Change had to have

Ⓑ Change look to looked

● Change greek to Greek

Ⓓ Make no change

Questions 9 – 16 pertain to the following passage:

Dogs in the Park

(1) On Saturday, my mom took me to a dog show at a park by our house. (2) The sun was out, and it was a really warm day. (3) I ride my bike to the park almost every day in the summer. (4) The dogs were all lying in the grass when we arrived, and they looked warm in the sun. (5) One of my mom's friends Mary, is a dog trainer, and she invited us to watch the dog show after my mom told her how much I love dogs.

(6) Their were all kinds of dogs at the show. (7) Some were really little, some were big, and some had really long hair. (8) My favorite were the dogs in the toy category and the sporting category. (9) The dogs that were waiting to be shown were with their trainers at different areas of the park getting ready. (10) Some trainers brushed its dog's hair, and some gave treats.

(11) We sat on the grass and watched the show. (12) The trainers were all dressed up. (13) The men wore suit pants and jackets, and the women wore dress skirts, stockings, and blazers. (14) All of the dogs were lined up and stood still wile the judges walked down and looked closely at all the dogs. (15) The judges looked at the dogs' hair, paws, and teeth. (16) Then it was time for each dog to show off. (17) Each trainer ran with their dog and held the leash high in the air. (18) The judges watched as the dogs ran, and judged how good they turned corners and listened to their trainers.

(19) At the end of the show, the judges awarded prizes. (20) The dogs and their trainers gathered in a line, and the judges presnted the winners with large ribbons. (21) Mary's dog won first place, and she was given a purple ribbon that was bigger than most of the small dogs in the toy category. (22) We left the park, and I told my mom that I want to learn how to train dogs.

9. **What change should be made in sentence 5?**

Ⓐ Change is to was

Ⓑ Delete the comma after Mary

Ⓒ Change invited to invites

Ⓓ Insert a comma after friends

10. **What change, if any, should be made in sentence 6?**

Ⓐ Change Their to There

Ⓑ Change dogs to dog's

Ⓒ Change were to was

Ⓓ Make no change

11. **What change, if any, should be made in sentence 8?**

Ⓐ Change were to was

Ⓑ Insert a comma after category

Ⓒ Change favorite to favorites

Ⓓ Make no change

12. **What change should be made in sentence 10?**

Ⓐ Change its to their

Ⓑ Change its to it's

Ⓒ Change brushed to brush

Ⓓ Change dog's to dogs

13. **What change should be made in sentence 14?**

Ⓐ Insert a comma after up

Ⓑ Change walked to walk

Ⓒ Change wile to while

Ⓓ Insert a comma after down

14. What change, if any, should be made in sentence 20?

Ⓐ Change dogs to dog

Ⓑ Change presnted to presented

Ⓒ Change their to its

Ⓓ Make no change

15. Which sentence does not belong in this essay?

Ⓐ Sentence 18

Ⓑ Sentence 11

Ⓒ Sentence 7

Ⓓ Sentence 3

16. What is the BEST transition word that could be added to the beginning of sentence 22?

Ⓐ However

Ⓑ Later

Ⓒ Otherwise

Ⓓ Consequentially

Questions 17 – 24 pertain to the following story:

First Party

(1) Today my brother turned one year old. (2) We had a big party to celebrate, and a lot of people came. (3) My ant came to the house early to help my mom hang streamers. (4) My cousin helped me make party favors for both the big kids and the babies. (5) We packed the little bags with candy, pencils, whistles, and noisemakers. (6) My parents invited a lot of people. (7) Soon the house was filled with family, friends, and even some babies for my brother to play with.

(8) My grandparents on my dad's side flew even flew in from California the day before to help. (9) My dad lighted the barbeque in the back yard and took orders from the guests. (10) He made hamburgers, turkey burgers, hot dogs, chicken wings, and sausages. (11) My aunt sliced strips of onion, tomato, pickles, and lettuce. (12) She also cuts up an avocado because she knows that it is my favorite topping on my hamburger. (13) My cousins, friends, and I all played in the backyard after we ate.

(14) My brother slept through most of the party, he was awake by the time he had cake. (15) He don't know he was missing his party by napping. (16)

My mom put him in his high chair, and we all sang "Happy birthday," to him. (17) There was one candle in the center of the large cake, and my mom blew it out since he was two little.

(18) My brother sat in his chair and ate cake. (19) Soon there was cake everywhere. (20) It was all over his hands, his face, his tabletop and chair. (21) There was blue icing everywhere. (22) He even lifted up his arms and grabbed pieces of his hair. (23) His big, blue eyes looked at everyone as they smiled and laughed. (24) He stuffed some more cake into his mouth and smiled. (25) I think he knew he had a good first birthday.

17. What change should be made in sentence 3?

Ⓐ Change hang to hanged

Ⓑ Change ant to aunt

Ⓒ Change help to helped

Ⓓ Change came to comes

18. Where is the best placement for sentence 8?

Ⓐ After sentence 2

Ⓑ After sentence 4

Ⓒ After sentence 5

Ⓓ No change is needed

19. What change, if any, should be made in sentence 9?

Ⓐ Change took to takes

Ⓑ Change barbeque to BBQ

Ⓒ Change lighted to lit

Ⓓ Make no change

20. What change, if any, should be made in sentence 12?

Ⓐ Change know to knew

Ⓑ Change cuts to cut

Ⓒ Change an to a

Ⓓ Make no change

21. **What is the BEST transition word that could be added to the beginning of sentence 14?**

Ⓐ Later

Ⓑ Therefore

Ⓒ Although

Ⓓ However

22. **What change, if any, should be made in sentence 15?**

Ⓐ Change don't to didn't

Ⓑ Change was to is

Ⓒ Change napping to nap

Ⓓ Make no change

23. **What change should be made in sentence 16?**

Ⓐ Change his to him

Ⓑ Change put to puts

Ⓒ Delete the quotation marks

Ⓓ Change birthday to Birthday

24. **What change should be made in sentence 17?**

Ⓐ Change There to They're

Ⓑ Delete the comma before and

Ⓒ Change blew to blowed

Ⓓ Change two to too

Questions 25 – 32 pertain to the passage:

Dinner is Served

(1) Every year my friend and I celebrate each other's birthdays by going out to dinner because our birthdays are three weeks apart. (2) On my birthday, my family took us to Aribba, my favorite mexican food restaurant. (3) For Annmae's birthday, she chose a Japanese restaurant called Tomo where the food is cooked at the table.

(4) I had never eaten Japanese food before and didn't know what to expect? (5) When the hostess brought us to our table, I was surprised to see that there were four extra seats. (6) That was not the only thing that was strange.

(7) The table was not a regular restaurant dinner table. (8) It was a half circle and there was a giant sheet of metal in the center. (9) The hostess came back with other people and sat them with us at our table.

(10) We filled out cards that said what kind of food we wanted. (11) We had to pick between chicken, beef, shrimp, and pork. (12) A man then came to our table and lit the metal sheet. (13) He laid out rice and vegetables, and started cutting and cooking. (14) He worked very fast it was almost hard for me to see his hands. (15) After the rice, he cooked each of the different meats and started serving plates. (16) While things were cooking he would take his spatula and fling a piece of bell pepper or carrot at someone at the table. (17) He toss the most at Annmae since it was her birthday, but they all hit her chin and slid down onto her shirt.

(18) It was really exciting watching our food cooked right in front of us. (19) The chef was nice and the food is delicious. (20) I even liked having other people sit at our table because it was like being at a party at dinner. (21) I am really glad that my friend chose Tomo and I can't wait to see where we try next year!

25. What change, if any, should be made in sentence 2?

Ⓐ Change birthday to birth day

Ⓑ Delete the comma after birthday

Ⓒ Change mexican to Mexican

Ⓓ Make no change

26. What change should be made in sentence 4?

Ⓐ Change had to have

Ⓑ Change Japanese to japanese

Ⓒ Change didn't to don't

Ⓓ Change the question mark to a period

27. What sentence could BEST follow and support sentence 9?

Ⓐ Now I understood why there were extra seats

Ⓑ The hostess smiled at us as she left

Ⓒ The woman worse a blue dress and he hair was tied back

Ⓓ I wondered how many times she was going to come back

28. What change, if any, should be made in sentence 10?

Ⓐ Change filled to filed

Ⓑ Change said to says

Ⓒ Change wanted to want

Ⓓ Make no change

29. What is the BEST way to revise sentence 14?

Ⓐ He worked very fast it was almost hard for me, to see his hands.

Ⓑ He worked very fast, and it was almost hard for me to see his hands.

Ⓒ His hands worked very fast it was almost hard for me to see.

Ⓓ Make no revision.

30. What change, if any, should be made in sentence 16?

Ⓐ Change were to are

Ⓑ Insert a comma after cooking

Ⓒ Change take to took

Ⓓ Make no change

31. What change, if any, should be made in sentence 17?

Ⓐ Delete the comma after birthday

Ⓑ Change hit to hitted

Ⓒ Change toss to tossed

Ⓓ Make no change

32. What change should be made in sentence 19?

Ⓐ Change is to was

Ⓑ Change was to is

Ⓒ Change delicious to deliciously

Ⓓ Change chef to Chef

Questions 33 – 40 pertain to the following passage:

History's Unsinkable Lessons

(1) In Ruth Campbell's book Exploring the Titanic, the events of the famous ship's only journey and sinking are brought to life. (2) In 1912, Titanic was built and was the largest passenger steamship at the time. (3) On what would be its first and only journey, the ship departed from Southampton in England and was supposed to arrive in New York City. (4) The ship hit an iceberg late at night on April 14, 1912, and sunked less than three hours later.

(5) Titanic was designed by some of the best engineers and had the latest technology of the time. (6) The ship was made to carry over three and a half thousand passengers and crew members, but had only twenty lifeboats. (7) There was not enough lifeboats for all of the people onboard, and as a result, only seven hundred six people survived.

(8) One interesting thing about Titanic, is that the ship was divided into classes. (9) The most expensive tickets were first class, and first class passengers had the biggest and much luxurious rooms. (10) The first class rooms were the closest to the ship's deck. (11) Because this the majority of survivors came from first class. (12) They were able to reach the deck fastest to get a seat on a lifeboat. (13) The third class rooms were located the farthest below deck, and the majority of the third class passengers did not survive.

(14) Ruth Campbell's book was very interesting but also sad because the story of Titanic is true. (15) However, Campbell ended the book by talking about the positive things that have happened because of this tragedy. (16) Most importantly, experts now recommend that ships' carry enough lifeboats for all passengers onboard. (17) This would have saved a lot of lifes. (18) It was a good book, and it displayed a good message in history that lessons should be learned from mistakes.

33. What change should be made in sentence 1?

Ⓐ Change ship's to ships

Ⓑ Insert a comma after book

Ⓒ Change are to is

Ⓓ Change brought to bring

34. **What change, if any, should be made in sentence 4?**

Ⓐ Change sunked to sank

Ⓑ Delete the comma after 14

Ⓒ Change hours to hour's

Ⓓ Make no change

35. **What change should be made in sentence 7?**

Ⓐ Change There to They're

Ⓑ Delete the comma after onboard

Ⓒ Change lifeboats to lifeboats'

Ⓓ Change was to were

36. **What change, if any, should be made in sentence 8?**

Ⓐ Change was to were

Ⓑ Delete the comma after Titanic

Ⓒ Change divided into divide

Ⓓ Make no change

37. **What is the BEST way to revise and combine sentence 11 and sentence 12?**

Ⓐ Because, the majority of survivors came from first class as they were able to reach the deck fastest to get a seat on a lifeboat

Ⓑ Because of this, the majority of survivors came from first class, as they were able to reach the deck fastest to get a seat on a lifeboat

Ⓒ Because this, the majority of survivors came from first class, they were able to reach the deck fastest to get a seat on a lifeboat

Ⓓ Because of this, the majority of survivors came from first class as they were able to reach the deck fastest to get a seat on a lifeboat

38. **What is the BEST transition word that could be added to the beginning of sentence 13?**

Ⓐ Lastly

Ⓑ However

Ⓒ Additionally

Ⓓ Therefore

39. What change should be made in sentence 16?

Ⓐ Change most important to importantist

Ⓑ Change found to find

Ⓒ Insert a comma after important

Ⓓ Change ship's to ships

40. What change, if any, should be made in sentence 17?

Ⓐ Change would have to would

Ⓑ Change a lot to a lot

Ⓒ Change lifes to lives

Ⓓ Make no change

Answers and Explanations

TEKS Standard §110.19(b)(14)(D) and (19)(A)(i)

1. B: because told is the correct past tense of the verb tell. Telled is not a word. A is not correct. When used as a noun, everyone is one word. C is not correct. Welcome is not a verb in this sentence and therefore does not need to be in the past tense like the rest of the essay.

TEKS Standard §110.19(14)(D) and (20)

2. D: because this sentence is a statement rather than a question. As a result, it should be punctuated with a period and not a question mark. A is not correct. Arrive is in the present tense, and the rest of the paragraph is in the past tense. B is not correct. Festival is not used in this sentence as a proper noun and therefore does not need to be capitalized. C is not correct. When we first arrived at the festival is an introductory clause, and a comma is needed after the introductory clause.

TEKS Standard §110.19(b)(14)(D) and (19)

3. A: because the subject of this sentence is favorite. Favorite is singular; therefore, the verb also must be singular in order for the subject and verb to agree. Were is plural. Was is singular. B is not correct. Mom's in this sentence is possessive and an apostrophe is needed. C is not correct. Loves is in the present tense, and the rest of the essay is in the past tense.

TEKS Standard §110.19(b)(14)(D) and (19)

4. A: because this is the simplest way to express the idea in a grammatically correct sentence. B is not correct, because this sentence is not grammatically correct. C is not correct, because the second sentence is a fragment.

TEKS Standard §110.19(b)(14)(D) and (19)

5. D: because it is the simplest way to express the idea in a grammatically correct sentence. A, B, and C are incorrect because these sentences are not grammatically correct. This sentence is not grammatically correct.

TEKS Standard §110.19(b)(14)(D) and (19)

6. B: because deliciously is an adverb rather than an adjective. It describes the noun, pitas, not the verb. A is not correct. Eat is in the present tense, and the rest of the essay is in the past tense. C is not correct. Two is spelled correctly and indicates the number. Too means "as well" or an indication of excess.

TEKS Standard §110.19(b)(14)(D) and (20)

7. C: because in this sentence dancers' is possessive and needs an apostrophe. Since dancers is plural, referring to more than one dancer, the apostrophe comes after the s. A is not correct. Cover is in the present tense, and the rest of the essay is in the past tense. B is not correct. The correct word is from, and it is spelled correctly.

TEKS Standard §110.19(b)(14)(D) and (20)(A)

8. C: It is correct because Greek is a proper noun and needs to be capitalized. A is not correct. Have is in the present tense, and the rest of the essay is in the past tense. B is not correct. A shift has occurred in the last sentence, and the second half of the sentence shifts into the present tense. The writer explains that she looks forward to the festival every year. Look in the present tense is therefore correct.

TEKS Standard §110.19(b)(14)(D) and (20)

9. D: It is correct because a comma is needed to separate the interjection of the name. A is not correct. Even though is is in the present tense and the rest of the essay is in the past tense, the sentence is describing a current person and should be in the present tense. B is not correct. A comma is needed to separate the interjection of the name. C is not correct. Invites is in the present tense and the rest of the essay, as a past event, is in the past tense.

TEKS Standard §110.19(b)(14)(D) and (21)

10. A: It is correct because a homonym has been misused. There is used to indicate a physical or abstract place. Their is used to indicate possession. B is not correct. In this sentence, dogs does not indicate possession and does not need an apostrophe. C is not correct. Was is in the present tense, and the rest of the essay is in the past tense.

TEKS Standard §110.19(b)(14)(D) and (19)

11. C: It is correct because the verb in the sentence, were, is plural, and the subject must be plural for subject-verb agreement. A is not correct. Was is in the present tense, and the rest of the essay is in the past tense. B is not correct. A comma is not needed because and the sporting category is not an independent clause.

TEKS Standard §110.19(b)(14)(D) and (19)

12. A: It is correct because there is plural and displays possession. Its is singular. The subject, trainers, is plural; therefore, the possession is plural as well. B is not correct. It's is only used as a contraction for it is, not for possession. C is not correct. Brush is in the present tense, and the rest of the essay is in the past tense. D is not correct. Dog's is possessive and needs an apostrophe.

TEKS Standard §110.19(b)(14)(D) and (21)

13. C: It is correct because a homonym has been misused. Wile means to trick or fool, and while indicates a period of time. A is not correct. A comma is not needed. No introductory clause or independent clauses need to be joined by a comma and conjunction. B is not correct. Walk is in the present tense and the rest of the essay is in the past tense. D is not correct. A comma is not needed. An independent clause does not follow the conjunction.

TEKS Standard §110.19(b)(14)(D) and (21)

14. B: It is correct because presented has been misspelled. A is not correct. Their trainers indicates that dogs should be plural, not singular. C is not correct. Their is plural and its is singular. The subject, dogs, is plural.

TEKS Standard §110.19(b)(14)(C)

15. D: It is correct because although this sentence provides new information, the content is not important to the rest of the essay. A, B, and C are because these sentences are important to the essay.

TEKS Standard §110.19(b)(19)(A)(viii)

16. B: It is correct because the opening phrase, We left the park, indicates a time lapse from the earlier events of the essay. An appropriate transition word would indicate time. A is not correct. However is not a good transition because sentence 22 is not contradicting anything in the previous sentence. C is not correct. Otherwise is not a good transition because sentence 22 does not suggest an alternate to something that occurred previously. D is not correct. Consequentially is not a good transition because the content of the sentence is not cause and effect from the previous sentence.

TEKS Standard §110.19(b)(14)(D) and (21)

17. B: It is correct because a homonym has been misused. Ant refers to an insect, and aunt refers to the sister of one's mother. A is not correct. Hang is not the verb of this sentence and does not need to be in the past tense. C is not correct. Help is not the verb of this sentence and does not need to be in the past tense. D is not correct. Came is the verb of this sentence. Comes is in the present tense and the rest of the essay is in the past tense.

TEKS Standard §110.19(b)(14)(B)

18. A: It is correct because the sentence discusses the grandparents traveling from California to help with the part. Therefore, this sentence should be placed after the description of the party and that a lot of people came. B is not correct. Sentence 4 discusses the cousin helping with party favors, and therefore a sentence about the grandparents' travel would not follow well.
C is not correct. Sentence 5 discusses the party favors, and therefore a sentence about the grandparents' travel would not follow well.

TEKS Standard §110.19(b)(19)(A)(i)

19. C: It is correct because lit is the correct past tense for the verb light. A is not correct. Takes is in the present tense and the rest of the essay is in the past tense. B is not correct. Barbeque is spelled correctly. BBQ is an abbreviation, not a word.

TEKS Standard §110.19(b)(19)(C)

20. B: It is correct because cuts is in the present tense, and the rest of the essay is in the past tense. Cut is in the past tense. A is not correct. Even though the essay is in the past tense, the act of the aunt knowing is a present and ongoing action and should be in the present tense. C is not correct. In this sentence, the article an is followed by a noun, avocado. Avocado begins with a vowel and a vowel sound; therefore, it needs to be introduced with the article an.

TEKS Standard §110.19(b)(19)(A)(viii)

21. C: It is correct because although means "in spite of" and is appropriate within the sentence. A is not correct. Later is not an appropriate transition word because it contradicts the beginning of the sentence. B is not correct. Therefore is not an appropriate transition word because there is no cause an effect from the previous sentence. D is not correct. However is not an appropriate transition word because sentence 14 does not contradict anything from the previous sentence.

TEKS Standard §110.19(b)(19)(C)

22. A: It is correct because don't is the conjunction of do not. Do not is in the present tense, and the rest of the essay is in the past tense. The past tense of do is did. B is not correct. Is is in the present tense, and the rest of the essay is in the past tense. C is not correct. Napping is a verb in this sentence, not a noun.

TEKS Standard §110.19(b)(20)(A)

23. D: It is correct because birthday is used as part of a song title. Song titles are proper nouns and need to be capitalized. A is not correct. His in this sentence indicates possession; him does not. B is not correct. Puts is in the present tense, and the rest of the essay is in the past tense. C is not correct. Quotations are needed around song titles.

TEKS Standard §110.19(b)(14)(D) and (21)

24. D: It is correct because a homonym has been misused. Two is the number. Too indicates "also," "excessively," or "very." A is not correct. There indicates location. They're is the contraction of there are. B is not correct. The sentence has two independent clauses joined by the conjunction and. A comma needs to be before the conjunction. H is not correct. Blew is the correct past tense of blow. Blowed is not a word.

TEKS Standard §110.19(b)(20)(A)

25. C: It is correct because Mexican is a proper noun, and proper nouns need to be capitalized. A is not correct. Birthday is one word. B is not correct. A comma is needed after an introductory clause.

TEKS Standard §110.19(b)(14)(D) and (20)

26. D: It is correct because the sentence is a statement, not a question, and needs a period as punctuation. A is not correct. Have is in the present tense, and the rest of the essay is in the past tense. B is not correct. Japanese is a proper noun and needs to be capitalized. C is not correct. Didn't is a contraction of did not and is in the past tense, like the rest of the essay. Don't is a contraction of do not and is in the present tense.

TEKS Standard §110.19(b)(14)(C) and (19)(A)(viii)

27. A: It is correct because the sentence both supports the previous sentences and provides additional information. Sentence 5 states that extra seats were available at the table. This sentence provides additional information that supports sentence 5 as well as sentence 9. B, C, and D are incorrect. Although these sentences provide new information, they do not link and support the previous sentences.

TEKS Standard §110.19(b)(14)(D)

28. D: It is correct because this sentence is grammatically correct. A is not correct. Within the context of the sentence, a card is filled out, not filed out. B is not correct. Says is in the present tense, and the rest of the essay is in the past tense. C is not correct. Want is in the present tense, and the rest of the essay is in the past tense.

TEKS Standard §110.19(b)(14)(D) and (19)

29. B: It is correct because it is the simplest way to express the idea in a grammatically correct sentence. A and C are not correct because these sentences are not grammatically correct.

TEKS Standard §110.19(b)(14)(D) and (20)(B)(i)

30. B: It is correct because While things were cooking is an introductory clause, and a comma is needed after the clause. A is not correct. Are is in the present tense and the rest of the essay is in the past tense. C is not correct. Take is part of would take and is in the past participle, not the present tense.

TEKS Standard §110.19(b)(19)(C)

31. The correct answer is **C.** It is correct because tossed is in the past tense, like the rest of the essay. Toss is in the present tense. A is not correct. A comma is needed before the conjunction when two independent clauses are joined by a conjunction. B is not correct. Hit is the correct past tense of hit. Hitted is not a word.

TEKS Standard §110.19(b)(19)(C)

32. A: It is correct because was is in the past tense, like the rest of the essay. Is is in the present tense. B is not correct. Is is in the present tense and the rest of the essay is in the past tense. C is not correct. Delicious is an adjective, not an adverb. It is used in this sentence to describe the noun, not the verb. D is not correct. Chef is not a proper noun and does not need to be capitalized.

TEKS Standard §110.19(b)(20)

33. B: It is correct because a comma is needed to separate the interjection of the book title. A is not correct. Ship in the sentence is possessive and requires the apostrophe. C is not correct. Are is the plural of is. The subject, events, is plural and therefore the verb needs to be plural in subject-verb agreement. D is not correct. Are brought is in the past participle, and bring is in the present tense.

TEKS Standard §110.19(b)(19)(A)(i)

34. A: It is correct because sank is the correct past tense of the verb sink. Sunked is not a word. B is not correct. A comma is needed to separate dates of the month from the year. H is not correct. Hours is not possessive and does not require the apostrophe.

TEKS Standard §110.19(b)(19)(A)(i)

35. D: It is correct because were is the plural past tense of is. The subject of the sentence, lifeboats, is plural, and the verb also must be plural in subject-verb agreement. A is not correct. There is used correctly. They're is a contraction of they are. B is not correct. A comma is needed to separate the interjection, and as a result. C is not correct. Lifeboats is not possessive and does not require the apostrophe.

TEKS Standard §110.19(b)(14)(D)

36. B: It is correct because there is no need for a comma. As it stands, the comma disrupts the normal flow of thought in the sentence. A is not correct. The subject, ship, is singular, and the verb also must be singular in subject-verb agreement. C is not correct. Was divided is in the past participle. Divide is in the present tense, and the rest of the essay is in the past.

TEKS Standard §110.19(b)(14)(C)

37. B: It is correct because it is the simplest way to express the idea in a grammatically correct sentence. Because of this refers to the content of the previous sentence. A is not correct. This sentence is not grammatically correct. C is not correct. This sentence is not grammatically correct. D is not correct. This sentence is not grammatically correct and needs a comma after class.

TEKS Standard §110.19(b)(19)(A)(viii)

38. C: It is correct because it connects the ideas from the previous sentence with the current sentence. The previous sentences explained the relationship between the locations of rooms to the deck with the survival rate of passengers. Sentence 13 provides additional information on this subject. A is not correct. Lastly is not an appropriate transition word as there was not a series of listed facts. B is not correct. However is not an appropriate transition word because sentence 13 is not contradicting anything from the previous sentence. D is not correct. Therefore is not an appropriate transition word because the new information does not involve cause and effect with the previous sentences.

TEKS Standard §110.19(b)(14)(D)

39. D: because in this sentence, ships is plural rather than possessive and does not require the apostrophe. A is not correct. Most important is correct. Importantist is not a word. B is not correct. Find is in the present tense and the rest of the essay is in the past tense. C is not correct, because the sentence does not need a comma. A comma would disrupt the normal flow of thought in the sentence.

TEKS Standard §110.19(b)(14)(D) and (21)

40. C: It is correct because lives is the correct plural of life. Lifes is not a word. A is not correct. Would have is in the past participle, and would is in the future tense. B is not correct. A lot is correct. Alot is not a word.

Sample Composition

Write a composition about a time in your life when you learned an important lesson.

It is a tradition in my family that we all go shopping for Thanksgiving together. Every year we buy two of everything. We buy two turkeys, two bags of potatoes, two pies, and lots of canned foods. My mom says it is important for us to go shopping as a family and really think about what we are buying. At the end of the shopping trip, we take half of the food, put it away in the house, and leave the other half in the car. Then we all get back into the car and Dad drives us to the homeless shelter. We give the shelter the rest of the food.

I did not want to go to the homeless shelter when I was younger. I wanted to stay at home and watch cartoons. I did not even want to go shopping for the food. I thought it was boring and that I had better things to do. My mom told me that I had to go and that it was very important. I remember my mom looking at the turkeys. She bought two of them. One was medium sized, and one was so big that she needed help putting it into the cart. "Go pick out some potatoes," she said to me. "And some green beans." I looked for a really long time to get the best green beans and potatoes for the shelter. It was fun to try to find the best.

When we got to the homeless shelter, people were lined up for over a block. They were all standing and wrapped in old blankets. I didn't understand. I asked my mom why they were lined up and why they were standing in the cold. She said that they did not live in a house like me and that they were lined up to get dinner for the night. She said that the shelter cooked dinner every night and gave it to the people who did not have any food or a place to live. My dad said that was why we were giving them food and why we had gone shopping. We were there so other people would have food to eat.

I now really look forward to going shopping for Thanksgiving. I try to pick the biggest turkey and the best potatoes. A few times a year my family cleans out our closets and gives old clothes, shoes, and blankets to the shelter. It still makes me sad to go to the shelter and see people standing in the cold and waiting for food, but I learned to be thankful for what I have and that it is really important to give to others.

Secret Key #1 - Time is Your Greatest Enemy

Pace Yourself

Wear a watch. At the beginning of the test, check the time (or start a chronometer on your watch to count the minutes), and check the time after every few questions to make sure you are "on schedule."

If you are forced to speed up, do it efficiently. Usually one or more answer choices can be eliminated without too much difficulty. Above all, don't panic. Don't speed up and just begin guessing at random choices. By pacing yourself, and continually monitoring your progress against your watch, you will always know exactly how far ahead or behind you are with your available time. If you find that you are one minute behind on the test, don't skip one question without spending any time on it, just to catch back up. Take 15 fewer seconds on the next four questions, and after four questions you'll have caught back up. Once you catch back up, you can continue working each problem at your normal pace.

Furthermore, don't dwell on the problems that you were rushed on. If a problem was taking up too much time and you made a hurried guess, it must be difficult. The difficult questions are the ones you are most likely to miss anyway, so it isn't a big loss. It is better to end with more time than you need than to run out of time.

Lastly, sometimes it is beneficial to slow down if you are constantly getting ahead of time. You are always more likely to catch a careless mistake by working more slowly than quickly, and among very high-scoring test takers (those who are likely to have lots of time left over), careless errors affect the score more than mastery of material.

Secret Key #2 - Guessing is not Guesswork

You probably know that guessing is a good idea - unlike other standardized tests, there is no penalty for getting a wrong answer. Even if you have no idea about a question, you still have a 20-25% chance of getting it right.

Most test takers do not understand the impact that proper guessing can have on their score. Unless you score extremely high, guessing will significantly contribute to your final score.

Monkeys Take the Test

What most test takers don't realize is that to insure that 20-25% chance, you have to guess randomly. If you put 20 monkeys in a room to take this test, assuming they answered once per question and behaved themselves, on average they would get 20-25% of the questions correct. Put 20 test takers in the room, and the average will be much lower among guessed questions. Why?

1. The test writers intentionally write deceptive answer choices that "look" right. A test taker has no idea about a question, so picks the "best looking" answer, which is often

wrong. The monkey has no idea what looks good and what doesn't, so will consistently be lucky about 20-25% of the time.

2. Test takers will eliminate answer choices from the guessing pool based on a hunch or intuition. Simple but correct answers often get excluded, leaving a 0% chance of being correct. The monkey has no clue, and often gets lucky with the best choice.

This is why the process of elimination endorsed by most test courses is flawed and detrimental to your performance- test takers don't guess, they make an ignorant stab in the dark that is usually worse than random.

$5 Challenge

Let me introduce one of the most valuable ideas of this course- the $5 challenge:

You only mark your "best guess" if you are willing to bet $5 on it.
You only eliminate choices from guessing if you are willing to bet $5 on it.

Why $5? Five dollars is an amount of money that is small yet not insignificant, and can really add up fast (20 questions could cost you $100). Likewise, each answer choice on one question of the test will have a small impact on your overall score, but it can really add up to a lot of points in the end.

The process of elimination IS valuable. The following shows your chance of guessing it right:

If you eliminate wrong answer choices until only this many remain:	Chance of getting it correct:
1	100%
2	50%
3	33%

However, if you accidentally eliminate the right answer or go on a hunch for an incorrect answer, your chances drop dramatically: to 0%. By guessing among all the answer choices, you are GUARANTEED to have a shot at the right answer.

That's why the $5 test is so valuable- if you give up the advantage and safety of a pure guess, it had better be worth the risk.

What we still haven't covered is how to be sure that whatever guess you make is truly random. Here's the easiest way:

Always pick the first answer choice among those remaining.

Such a technique means that you have decided, **before you see a single test question**, exactly how you are going to guess- and since the order of choices tells you nothing about which one is correct, this guessing technique is perfectly random.

This section is not meant to scare you away from making educated guesses or eliminating choices- you just need to define when a choice is worth eliminating. The $5 test, along with a pre-defined random guessing strategy, is the best way to make sure you reap all of the benefits of guessing.

Secret Key #3 - Practice Smarter, Not Harder

Many test takers delay the test preparation process because they dread the awful amounts of practice time they think necessary to succeed on the test. We have refined an effective method that will take you only a fraction of the time.

There are a number of "obstacles" in your way to succeed. Among these are answering questions, finishing in time, and mastering test-taking strategies. All must be executed on the day of the test at peak performance, or your score will suffer. The test is a mental marathon that has a large impact on your future.

Just like a marathon runner, it is important to work your way up to the full challenge. So first you just worry about questions, and then time, and finally strategy:

Success Strategy

1. Find a good source for practice tests.
2. If you are willing to make a larger time investment, consider using more than one study guide- often the different approaches of multiple authors will help you "get" difficult concepts.
3. Take a practice test with no time constraints, with all study helps "open book." Take your time with questions and focus on applying strategies.
4. Take a practice test with time constraints, with all guides "open book."
5. Take a final practice test with no open material and time limits

If you have time to take more practice tests, just repeat step 5. By gradually exposing yourself to the full rigors of the test environment, you will condition your mind to the stress of test day and maximize your success.

Secret Key #4 - Prepare, Don't Procrastinate

Let me state an obvious fact: if you take the test three times, you will get three different scores. This is due to the way you feel on test day, the level of preparedness you have, and, despite the test writers' claims to the contrary, some tests WILL be easier for you than others.

Since your future depends so much on your score, you should maximize your chances of success. In order to maximize the likelihood of success, you've got to prepare in advance. This means taking practice tests and spending time learning the information and test taking strategies you will need to succeed.

Never take the test as a "practice" test, expecting that you can just take it again if you need to. Feel free to take sample tests on your own, but when you go to take the official test, be prepared, be focused, and do your best the first time!

Secret Key #5 - Test Yourself

Everyone knows that time is money. There is no need to spend too much of your time or too little of your time preparing for the test. You should only spend as much of your precious time preparing as is necessary for you to get the score you need.

Once you have taken a practice test under real conditions of time constraints, then you will know if you are ready for the test or not.

If you have scored extremely high the first time that you take the practice test, then there is not much point in spending countless hours studying. You are already there.

Benchmark your abilities by retaking practice tests and seeing how much you have improved. Once you score high enough to guarantee success, then you are ready.

If you have scored well below where you need, then knuckle down and begin studying in earnest. Check your improvement regularly through the use of practice tests under real conditions. Above all, don't worry, panic, or give up The key is perseverance!

Then, when you go to take the test, remain confident and remember how well you did on the practice tests. If you can score high enough on a practice test, then you can do the same on the real thing.

General Strategies

The most important thing you can do is to ignore your fears and jump into the test immediately- do not be overwhelmed by any strange-sounding terms. You have to jump into the test like jumping into a pool- all at once is the easiest way.

Make Predictions

As you read and understand the question, try to guess what the answer will be. Remember that several of the answer choices are wrong, and once you begin reading them, your mind will immediately become cluttered with answer choices designed to throw you off. Your mind is typically the most focused immediately after you have read the question and digested its contents. If you can, try to predict what the correct answer will be. You may be surprised at what you can predict.

Quickly scan the choices and see if your prediction is in the listed answer choices. If it is, then you can be quite confident that you have the right answer. It still won't hurt to check the other answer choices, but most of the time, you've got it!

Answer the Question

It may seem obvious to only pick answer choices that answer the question, but the test writers can create some excellent answer choices that are wrong. Don't pick an answer just because it sounds right, or you believe it to be true. It MUST answer the question. Once you've made your selection, always go back and check it against the question and make sure that you didn't misread the question, and the answer choice does answer the question posed.

Benchmark

After you read the first answer choice, decide if you think it sounds correct or not. If it doesn't, move on to the next answer choice. If it does, mentally mark that answer choice. This doesn't mean that you've definitely selected it as your answer choice, it just means that it's the best you've seen thus far. Go ahead and read the next choice. If the next choice is worse than the one you've already selected, keep going to the next answer choice. If the next choice is better than the choice you've already selected, mentally mark the new answer choice as your best guess.

The first answer choice that you select becomes your standard. Every other answer choice must be benchmarked against that standard. That choice is correct until proven otherwise by another answer choice beating it out. Once you've decided that no other answer choice seems as good, do one final check to ensure that your answer choice answers the question posed.

Valid Information

Don't discount any of the information provided in the question. Every piece of information may be necessary to determine the correct answer. None of the information in the question is there to throw you off (while the answer choices will certainly have information to throw you off). If two seemingly unrelated topics are discussed, don't ignore either. You can be confident there is a relationship, or it wouldn't be included in the question, and you are probably going to have to determine what is that relationship to find the answer.

Avoid "Fact Traps"

Don't get distracted by a choice that is factually true. Your search is for the answer that answers the question. Stay focused and don't fall for an answer that is true but incorrect. Always go back to the question and make sure you're choosing an answer that actually answers the question and is not just a true statement. An answer can be factually correct, but it MUST answer the question asked. Additionally, two answers can both be seemingly correct, so be sure to read all of the answer choices, and make sure that you get the one that BEST answers the question.

Milk the Question

Some of the questions may throw you completely off. They might deal with a subject you have not been exposed to, or one that you haven't reviewed in years. While your lack of knowledge about the subject will be a hindrance, the question itself can give you many clues that will help you find the correct answer. Read the question carefully and look for clues. Watch particularly for adjectives and nouns describing difficult terms or words that you don't recognize. Regardless of if you completely understand a word or not, replacing it with a synonym either provided or one you more familiar with may help you to understand what the questions are asking. Rather than wracking your mind about specific detailed information concerning a difficult term or word, try to use mental substitutes that are easier to understand.

The Trap of Familiarity

Don't just choose a word because you recognize it. On difficult questions, you may not recognize a number of words in the answer choices. The test writers don't put "make-believe" words on the test; so don't think that just because you only recognize all the words in one answer choice means that answer choice must be correct. If you only recognize words in one answer choice, then focus on that one. Is it correct? Try your best to determine if it is correct. If it is, that is great, but if it doesn't, eliminate it. Each word and answer choice you eliminate increases your chances of getting the question correct, even if you then have to guess among the unfamiliar choices.

Eliminate Answers

Eliminate choices as soon as you realize they are wrong. But be careful! Make sure you consider all of the possible answer choices. Just because one appears right, doesn't mean that the next one won't be even better! The test writers will usually put more than one good answer choice for every question, so read all of them. Don't worry if you are stuck between two that seem right. By getting down to just two remaining possible choices, your odds are now 50/50. Rather than wasting too much time, play the odds. You are guessing, but guessing wisely, because you've been able to knock out some of the answer choices that you know are wrong. If you are eliminating choices and realize that the last answer choice you are left with is also obviously wrong, don't panic. Start over and consider each choice again. There may easily be something that you missed the first time and will realize on the second pass.

Tough Questions

If you are stumped on a problem or it appears too hard or too difficult, don't waste time. Move on! Remember though, if you can quickly check for obviously incorrect answer choices, your chances of guessing correctly are greatly improved. Before you completely give up, at least try to knock out a couple of possible answers. Eliminate what you can and then guess at the remaining answer choices before moving on.

Brainstorm

If you get stuck on a difficult question, spend a few seconds quickly brainstorming. Run through the complete list of possible answer choices. Look at each choice and ask yourself, "Could this answer the question satisfactorily?" Go through each answer choice and consider it independently of the other. By systematically going through all possibilities, you may find something that you would otherwise overlook. Remember that when you get stuck, it's important to try to keep moving.

Read Carefully

Understand the problem. Read the question and answer choices carefully. Don't miss the question because you misread the terms. You have plenty of time to read each question thoroughly and make sure you understand what is being asked. Yet a happy medium must be attained, so don't waste too much time. You must read carefully, but efficiently.

Face Value

When in doubt, use common sense. Always accept the situation in the problem at face value. Don't read too much into it. These problems will not require you to make huge leaps of logic. The test writers aren't trying to throw you off with a cheap trick. If you have to go beyond creativity and make a leap of logic in order to have an answer choice answer the question, then you should look at the other answer choices. Don't overcomplicate the problem by creating theoretical relationships or explanations that will warp time or space. These are normal problems rooted in reality. It's just that the applicable relationship or explanation may not be readily apparent and you have to figure things out. Use your common sense to interpret anything that isn't clear.

Prefixes

If you're having trouble with a word in the question or answer choices, try dissecting it. Take advantage of every clue that the word might include. Prefixes and suffixes can be a huge help. Usually they allow you to determine a basic meaning. Pre- means before, post- means after, pro - is positive, de- is negative. From these prefixes and suffixes, you can get an idea of the general meaning of the word and try to put it into context. Beware though of any traps. Just because con is the opposite of pro, doesn't necessarily mean congress is the opposite of progress!

Hedge Phrases

Watch out for critical "hedge" phrases, such as likely, may, can, will often, sometimes, often, almost, mostly, usually, generally, rarely, sometimes. Question writers insert these hedge phrases to cover every possibility. Often an answer choice will be wrong simply because it leaves no room for exception. Avoid answer choices that have definitive words like "exactly," and "always".

Switchback Words

Stay alert for "switchbacks". These are the words and phrases frequently used to alert you to shifts in thought. The most common switchback word is "but". Others include although, however, nevertheless, on the other hand, even though, while, in spite of, despite, regardless of.

New Information

Correct answer choices will rarely have completely new information included. Answer choices typically are straightforward reflections of the material asked about and will directly relate to the question. If a new piece of information is included in an answer choice that doesn't even seem to relate to the topic being asked about, then that answer choice is likely incorrect. All of the information needed to answer the question is usually provided for you, and so you should not have to make guesses that are unsupported or choose answer choices that require unknown information that cannot be reasoned on its own.

Time Management

On technical questions, don't get lost on the technical terms. Don't spend too much time on any one question. If you don't know what a term means, then since you don't have a dictionary, odds are you aren't going to get much further. You should immediately recognize terms as whether or not you know them. If you don't, work with the other clues that you have, the other answer choices and terms provided, but don't waste too much time trying to figure out a difficult term.

Contextual Clues

Look for contextual clues. An answer can be right but not correct. The contextual clues will help you find the answer that is most right and is correct. Understand the context in which a phrase or statement is made. This will help you make important distinctions.

Don't Panic

Panicking will not answer any questions for you. Therefore, it isn't helpful. When you first see the question, if your mind goes blank, take a deep breath. Force yourself to mechanically go through the steps of solving the problem and using the strategies you've learned.

Pace Yourself

Don't get clock fever. It's easy to be overwhelmed when you're looking at a page full of questions, your mind is full of random thoughts and feeling confused, and the clock is ticking down faster than you would like. Calm down and maintain the pace that you have set for yourself. As long as you are on track by monitoring your pace, you are guaranteed to have enough time for yourself. When you get to the last few minutes of the test, it may seem like you won't have enough time left, but if you only have as many questions as you should have left at that point, then you're right on track!

Answer Selection

The best way to pick an answer choice is to eliminate all of those that are wrong, until only one is left and confirm that is the correct answer. Sometimes though, an answer choice may immediately look right. Be careful! Take a second to make sure that the other choices are not equally obvious. Don't make a hasty mistake. There are only two times that you should stop before checking other answers. First is when you are positive that the answer choice you have selected is correct. Second is when time is almost out and you have to make a quick guess!

Check Your Work

Since you will probably not know every term listed and the answer to every question, it is important that you get credit for the ones that you do know. Don't miss any questions through careless mistakes. If at all possible, try to take a second to look back over your answer selection and make sure you've selected the correct answer choice and haven't made a costly careless mistake (such as marking an answer choice that you didn't mean to mark). This quick double check should more than pay for itself in caught mistakes for the time it costs.

Beware of Directly Quoted Answers

Sometimes an answer choice will repeat word for word a portion of the question or reference section. However, beware of such exact duplication – it may be a trap! More than likely, the correct choice will paraphrase or summarize a point, rather than being exactly the same wording.

Slang

Scientific sounding answers are better than slang ones. An answer choice that begins "To compare the outcomes..." is much more likely to be correct than one that begins "Because some people insisted..."

Extreme Statements

Avoid wild answers that throw out highly controversial ideas that are proclaimed as established fact. An answer choice that states the "process should be used in certain situations, if..." is much more likely to be correct than one that states the "process should be discontinued completely." The first is a calm rational statement and doesn't even make a definitive, uncompromising stance, using a hedge word "if" to provide wiggle room, whereas the second choice is a radical idea and far more extreme.

Answer Choice Families

When you have two or more answer choices that are direct opposites or parallels, one of them is usually the correct answer. For instance, if one answer choice states "x increases" and another answer choice states "x decreases" or "y increases," then those two or three answer choices are very similar in construction and fall into the same family of answer choices. A family of answer choices is when two or three answer choices are very similar in construction, and yet often have a directly opposite meaning. Usually the correct answer choice will be in that family of answer choices. The "odd man out" or answer choice that doesn't seem to fit the parallel construction of the other answer choices is more likely to be incorrect.

Top 20 Test Taking Tips

1. Carefully follow all the test registration procedures
2. Know the test directions, duration, topics, question types, how many questions
3. Setup a flexible study schedule at least 3-4 weeks before test day
4. Study during the time of day you are most alert, relaxed, and stress free
5. Maximize your learning style; visual learner use visual study aids, auditory learner use auditory study aids
6. Focus on your weakest knowledge base
7. Find a study partner to review with and help clarify questions
8. Practice, practice, practice
9. Get a good night's sleep; don't try to cram the night before the test
10. Eat a well balanced meal
11. Know the exact physical location of the testing site; drive the route to the site prior to test day
12. Bring a set of ear plugs; the testing center could be noisy
13. Wear comfortable, loose fitting, layered clothing to the testing center; prepare for it to be either cold or hot during the test
14. Bring at least 2 current forms of ID to the testing center
15. Arrive to the test early; be prepared to wait and be patient
16. Eliminate the obviously wrong answer choices, then guess the first remaining choice
17. Pace yourself; don't rush, but keep working and move on if you get stuck
18. Maintain a positive attitude even if the test is going poorly
19. Keep your first answer unless you are positive it is wrong
20. Check your work, don't make a careless mistake

Special Report: What Your Test Score Will Tell You About Your IQ

Did you know that most standardized tests correlate very strongly with IQ? In fact, your general intelligence is a better predictor of your success than any other factor, and most tests intentionally measure this trait to some degree to ensure that those selected by the test are truly qualified for the test's purposes.

Before we can delve into the relation between your test score and IQ, I will first have to explain what exactly is IQ. Here's the formula:

Your IQ = 100 + (Number of standard deviations below or above the average)*15

Now, let's define standard deviations by using an example. If we have 5 people with 5 different heights, then first we calculate the average. Let's say the average was 65 inches. The standard deviation is the "average distance" away from the average of each of the members. It is a direct measure of variability - if the 5 people included Jackie Chan and Shaquille O'Neal, obviously there's a lot more variability in that group than a group of 5 sisters who are all within 6 inches in height of each other. The standard deviation uses a number to characterize the average range of difference within a group.

A convenient feature of most groups is that they have a "normal" distribution- makes sense that most things would be normal, right? Without getting into a bunch of statistical mumbo-jumbo, you just need to know that if you know the average of the group and the standard deviation, you can successfully predict someone's percentile rank in the group.

Confused? Let me give you an example. If instead of 5 people's heights, we had 100 people, we could figure out their rank in height JUST by knowing the average, standard deviation, and their height. We wouldn't need to know each person's height and manually rank them, we could just predict their rank based on three numbers.

What this means is that you can take your PERCENTILE rank that is often given with your test and relate this to your RELATIVE IQ of people taking the test - that is, your IQ relative to the people taking the test. Obviously, there's no way to know your actual IQ because the people taking a standardized test are usually not very good samples of the general population- many of those with extremely low IQ's never achieve a level of success or competency necessary to complete a typical standardized test. In fact, professional psychologists who measure IQ actually have to use non-written tests that can fairly measure the IQ of those not able to complete a traditional test.

The bottom line is to not take your test score too seriously, but it is fun to compute your "relative IQ" among the people who took the test with you. I've done the calculations below. Just look up your percentile rank in the left and then you'll see your "relative IQ" for your test in the right hand column-

Percentile Rank	Your Relative IQ		Percentile Rank	Your Relative IQ
99	135		59	103
98	131		58	103
97	128		57	103
96	126		56	102
95	125		55	102
94	123		54	102
93	122		53	101
92	121		52	101
91	120		51	100
90	119		50	100
89	118		49	100
88	118		48	99
87	117		47	99
86	116		46	98
85	116		45	98
84	115		44	98
83	114		43	97
82	114		42	97
81	113		41	97
80	113		40	96
79	112		39	96
78	112		38	95
77	111		37	95
76	111		36	95
75	110		35	94
74	110		34	94
73	109		33	93
72	109		32	93
71	108		31	93
70	108		30	92
69	107		29	92
68	107		28	91
67	107		27	91
66	106		26	90
65	106		25	90
64	105		24	89
63	105		23	89
62	105		22	88
61	104		21	88
60	104		20	87

Special Report: What is Test Anxiety and How to Overcome It?

The very nature of tests caters to some level of anxiety, nervousness or tension, just as we feel for any important event that occurs in our lives. A little bit of anxiety or nervousness can be a good thing. It helps us with motivation, and makes achievement just that much sweeter. However, too much anxiety can be a problem; especially if it hinders our ability to function and perform.

"Test anxiety," is the term that refers to the emotional reactions that some test-takers experience when faced with a test or exam. Having a fear of testing and exams is based upon a rational fear, since the test-taker's performance can shape the course of an academic career. Nevertheless, experiencing excessive fear of examinations will only interfere with the test-takers ability to perform, and his/her chances to be successful.

There are a large variety of causes that can contribute to the development and sensation of test anxiety. These include, but are not limited to lack of performance and worrying about issues surrounding the test.

Lack of Preparation

Lack of preparation can be identified by the following behaviors or situations:

Not scheduling enough time to study, and therefore cramming the night before the test or exam
Managing time poorly, to create the sensation that there is not enough time to do everything
Failing to organize the text information in advance, so that the study material consists of the entire text and not simply the pertinent information
Poor overall studying habits

Worrying, on the other hand, can be related to both the test taker, or many other factors around him/her that will be affected by the results of the test. These include worrying about:

Previous performances on similar exams, or exams in general
How friends and other students are achieving
The negative consequences that will result from a poor grade or failure

There are three primary elements to test anxiety. Physical components, which involve the same typical bodily reactions as those to acute anxiety (to be discussed below). Emotional factors have to do with fear or panic. Mental or cognitive issues concerning attention spans and memory abilities.

Physical Signals

There are many different symptoms of test anxiety, and these are not limited to mental and emotional strain. Frequently there are a range of physical signals that will let a test taker know that he/she is suffering from test anxiety. These bodily changes can include the following:

Perspiring
Sweaty palms
Wet, trembling hands
Nausea
Dry mouth
A knot in the stomach
Headache
Faintness
Muscle tension
Aching shoulders, back and neck
Rapid heart beat
Feeling too hot/cold

To recognize the sensation of test anxiety, a test-taker should monitor him/herself for the following sensations:

The physical distress symptoms as listed above
Emotional sensitivity, expressing emotional feelings such as the need to cry or laugh too much, or a sensation of anger or helplessness
A decreased ability to think, causing the test-taker to blank out or have racing thoughts that are hard to organize or control.

Though most students will feel some level of anxiety when faced with a test or exam, the majority can cope with that anxiety and maintain it at a manageable level. However, those who cannot are faced with a very real and very serious condition, which can and should be controlled for the immeasurable benefit of this sufferer.

Naturally, these sensations lead to negative results for the testing experience. The most common effects of test anxiety have to do with nervousness and mental blocking.

Nervousness

Nervousness can appear in several different levels:

The test-taker's difficulty, or even inability to read and understand the questions on the test
The difficulty or inability to organize thoughts to a coherent form
The difficulty or inability to recall key words and concepts relating to the testing questions (especially essays)
The receipt of poor grades on a test, though the test material was well known by the test taker

Conversely, a person may also experience mental blocking, which involves:

Blanking out on test questions
Only remembering the correct answers to the questions when the test has already finished.

Fortunately for test anxiety sufferers, beating these feelings, to a large degree, has to do with proper preparation. When a test taker has a feeling of preparedness, then anxiety will be dramatically lessened.

The first step to resolving anxiety issues is to distinguish which of the two types of anxiety are being suffered. If the anxiety is a direct result of a lack of preparation, this should be considered a normal reaction, and the anxiety level (as opposed to the test results) shouldn't be anything to worry about. However, if, when adequately prepared, the test-taker still panics, blanks out, or seems to overreact, this is not a fully rational reaction. While this can be considered normal too, there are many ways to combat and overcome these effects.

Remember that anxiety cannot be entirely eliminated, however, there are ways to minimize it, to make the anxiety easier to manage. Preparation is one of the best ways to minimize test anxiety. Therefore the following techniques are wise in order to best fight off any anxiety that may want to build.

To begin with, try to avoid cramming before a test, whenever it is possible. By trying to memorize an entire term's worth of information in one day, you'll be shocking your system, and not giving yourself a very good chance to absorb the information. This is an easy path to anxiety, so for those who suffer from test anxiety, cramming should not even be considered an option.

Instead of cramming, work throughout the semester to combine all of the material which is presented throughout the semester, and work on it gradually as the course goes by, making sure to master the main concepts first, leaving minor details for a week or so before the test.

To study for the upcoming exam, be sure to pose questions that may be on the examination, to gauge the ability to answer them by integrating the ideas from your texts, notes and lectures, as well as any supplementary readings.

If it is truly impossible to cover all of the information that was covered in that particular term, concentrate on the most important portions, that can be covered very well. Learn these concepts as best as possible, so that when the test comes, a goal can be made to use these concepts as presentations of your knowledge.

In addition to study habits, changes in attitude are critical to beating a struggle with test anxiety. In fact, an improvement of the perspective over the entire test-taking experience can actually help a test taker to enjoy studying and therefore improve the overall experience. Be certain not to overemphasize the significance of the grade - know that the result of the test is neither a reflection of self worth, nor is it a measure of intelligence; one grade will not predict a person's future success.

To improve an overall testing outlook, the following steps should be tried:

Keeping in mind that the most reasonable expectation for taking a test is to expect to try to demonstrate as much of what you know as you possibly can.
Reminding ourselves that a test is only one test; this is not the only one, and there will be others.
The thought of thinking of oneself in an irrational, all-or-nothing term should be avoided at all costs.
A reward should be designated for after the test, so there's something to look forward to. Whether it be going to a movie, going out to eat, or simply visiting friends, schedule it in advance, and do it no matter what result is expected on the exam.

Test-takers should also keep in mind that the basics are some of the most important things, even beyond anti-anxiety techniques and studying. Never neglect the basic social, emotional and biological needs, in order to try to absorb information. In order to best achieve, these three factors must be held as just as important as the studying itself.

Study Steps

Remember the following important steps for studying:

Maintain healthy nutrition and exercise habits. Continue both your recreational activities and social pass times. These both contribute to your physical and emotional well being.
Be certain to get a good amount of sleep, especially the night before the test, because when you're overtired you are not able to perform to the best of your best ability.
Keep the studying pace to a moderate level by taking breaks when they are needed, and varying the work whenever possible, to keep the mind fresh instead of getting bored.
When enough studying has been done that all the material that can be learned has been learned, and the test taker is prepared for the test, stop studying and do something relaxing such as listening to music, watching a movie, or taking a warm bubble bath.

There are also many other techniques to minimize the uneasiness or apprehension that is experienced along with test anxiety before, during, or even after the examination. In fact, there are a great deal of things that can be done to stop anxiety from interfering with lifestyle and performance. Again, remember that anxiety will not be eliminated entirely, and it shouldn't be. Otherwise that "up" feeling for exams would not exist, and most of us depend on that sensation to perform better than usual. However, this anxiety has to be at a level that is manageable.

Of course, as we have just discussed, being prepared for the exam is half the battle right away. Attending all classes, finding out what knowledge will be expected on the exam, and knowing the exam schedules are easy steps to lowering anxiety. Keeping up with work will remove the need to cram, and efficient study habits will eliminate wasted time. Studying should be done in an ideal location for concentration, so that it is simple to become interested in the material and give it complete attention. A method such as SQ3R (Survey, Question, Read, Recite, Review) is a wonderful key to follow to make sure that the study habits are as effective as possible, especially in the case of learning from a textbook. Flashcards are great techniques for memorization. Learning to take good notes will mean that notes will be full of useful information, so that less sifting will need to be done to seek out what is pertinent for studying. Reviewing notes after class and then again on occasion will keep the information fresh in the mind. From notes that have been taken summary sheets and outlines can be made for simpler reviewing.

A study group can also be a very motivational and helpful place to study, as there will be a sharing of ideas, all of the minds can work together, to make sure that everyone understands, and the studying will be made more interesting because it will be a social occasion.

Basically, though, as long as the test-taker remains organized and self confident, with efficient study habits, less time will need to be spent studying, and higher grades will be achieved.

To become self confident, there are many useful steps. The first of these is "self talk." It has been shown through extensive research, that self-talk for students who suffer from test anxiety, should be well monitored, in order to make sure that it contributes to self confidence as opposed to sinking the student. Frequently the self talk of test-anxious students is negative or self-defeating, thinking that everyone else is smarter and faster, that they always mess up, and that if they don't do well, they'll fail the entire course. It is important to decreasing anxiety that awareness is made of self talk. Try writing any negative self thoughts and then disputing them with a positive statement instead. Begin self-encouragement as though it was a friend speaking. Repeat positive statements to help reprogram the mind to believing in successes instead of failures.

Helpful Techniques

Other extremely helpful techniques include:

Self-visualization of doing well and reaching goals
While aiming for an "A" level of understanding, don't try to "overprotect" by setting your expectations lower. This will only convince the mind to stop studying in order to meet the lower expectations.
Don't make comparisons with the results or habits of other students. These are individual factors, and different things work for different people, causing different results.
Strive to become an expert in learning what works well, and what can be done in order to improve. Consider collecting this data in a journal.
Create rewards for after studying instead of doing things before studying that will only turn into avoidance behaviors.
Make a practice of relaxing - by using methods such as progressive relaxation, self-hypnosis, guided imagery, etc - in order to make relaxation an automatic sensation.
Work on creating a state of relaxed concentration so that concentrating will take on the focus of the mind, so that none will be wasted on worrying.
Take good care of the physical self by eating well and getting enough sleep.
Plan in time for exercise and stick to this plan.

Beyond these techniques, there are other methods to be used before, during and after the test that will help the test-taker perform well in addition to overcoming anxiety.

Before the exam comes the academic preparation. This involves establishing a study schedule and beginning at least one week before the actual date of the test. By doing this, the anxiety of not having enough time to study for the test will be automatically eliminated. Moreover, this will make the studying a much more effective experience, ensuring that the learning will be an easier process. This relieves much undue pressure on the test-taker.

Summary sheets, note cards, and flash cards with the main concepts and examples of these main concepts should be prepared in advance of the actual studying time. A topic should never be eliminated from this process. By omitting a topic because it isn't expected to be on the test is only setting up the test-taker for anxiety should it actually appear on the exam. Utilize the course syllabus for laying out the topics that should be studied. Carefully go over the notes that were made in class, paying special attention to any of the issues that the professor took special care to emphasize while lecturing in class. In the textbooks, use the chapter review, or if possible, the chapter tests, to begin your review.

It may even be possible to ask the instructor what information will be covered on the exam, or what the format of the exam will be (for example, multiple choice, essay, free form, true-false). Additionally, see if it is possible to find out how many questions will be on the test. If a review sheet or sample test has been offered by the professor, make good use of it, above anything else, for the preparation for the test. Another great resource for getting to know the examination is reviewing tests from previous semesters. Use these tests to review, and aim to achieve a 100% score on each of the possible topics. With a few exceptions, the goal that you set for yourself is the highest one that you will reach.

Take all of the questions that were assigned as homework, and rework them to any other possible course material. The more problems reworked, the more skill and confidence will form as a result. When forming the solution to a problem, write out each of the steps. Don't simply do head work. By doing as many steps on paper as possible, much clarification and therefore confidence will be formed. Do this with as many homework problems as possible, before checking the answers. By checking the answer after each problem, a reinforcement will exist, that will not be on the exam. Study situations should be as exam-like as possible, to prime the test-taker's system for the experience. By waiting to check the answers at the end, a psychological advantage will be formed, to decrease the stress factor.

Another fantastic reason for not cramming is the avoidance of confusion in concepts, especially when it comes to mathematics. 8-10 hours of study will become one hundred percent more effective if it is spread out over a week or at least several days, instead of doing it all in one sitting. Recognize that the human brain requires time in order to assimilate new material, so frequent breaks and a span of study time over several days will be much more beneficial.

Additionally, don't study right up until the point of the exam. Studying should stop a minimum of one hour before the exam begins. This allows the brain to rest and put things in their proper order. This will also provide the time to become as relaxed as possible when going into the examination room. The test-taker will also have time to eat well and eat sensibly. Know that the brain needs food as much as the rest of the body. With enough food and enough sleep, as well as a relaxed attitude, the body and the mind are primed for success.

Avoid any anxious classmates who are talking about the exam. These students only spread anxiety, and are not worth sharing the anxious sentimentalities.

Before the test also involves creating a positive attitude, so mental preparation should also be a point of concentration. There are many keys to creating a positive attitude. Should fears become rushing in, make a visualization of taking the exam, doing well, and seeing an A written on the paper. Write out a list of affirmations that will bring a feeling of confidence, such as "I am doing well in my English class," "I studied well and know my material," "I enjoy this class." Even if the affirmations aren't believed at first, it sends a positive message to the subconscious which will result in an alteration of the overall belief system, which is the system that creates reality.

If a sensation of panic begins, work with the fear and imagine the very worst! Work through the entire scenario of not passing the test, failing the entire course, and dropping out of school, followed by not getting a job, and pushing a shopping cart through the dark alley where you'll live. This will place things into perspective! Then, practice deep breathing and create a visualization of the opposite situation - achieving an "A" on the exam, passing the entire course, receiving the degree at a graduation ceremony.

On the day of the test, there are many things to be done to ensure the best results, as well as the most calm outlook. The following stages are suggested in order to maximize test-taking potential:

Begin the examination day with a moderate breakfast, and avoid any coffee or beverages with caffeine if the test taker is prone to jitters. Even people who are used to managing caffeine can feel jittery or light-headed when it is taken on a test day.
Attempt to do something that is relaxing before the examination begins. As last minute cramming clouds the mastering of overall concepts, it is better to use this time to create a calming outlook.
Be certain to arrive at the test location well in advance, in order to provide time to select a location that is away from doors, windows and other distractions, as well as giving enough time to relax before the test begins.
Keep away from anxiety generating classmates who will upset the sensation of stability and relaxation that is being attempted before the exam.
Should the waiting period before the exam begins cause anxiety, create a self-distraction by reading a light magazine or something else that is relaxing and simple.

During the exam itself, read the entire exam from beginning to end, and find out how much time should be allotted to each individual problem. Once writing the exam, should more time be taken for a problem, it should be abandoned, in order to begin another problem. If there is time at the end, the unfinished problem can always be returned to and completed.

Read the instructions very carefully - twice - so that unpleasant surprises won't follow during or after the exam has ended.

When writing the exam, pretend that the situation is actually simply the completion of homework within a library, or at home. This will assist in forming a relaxed atmosphere, and will allow the brain extra focus for the complex thinking function.

Begin the exam with all of the questions with which the most confidence is felt. This will build the confidence level regarding the entire exam and will begin a quality momentum. This will also create encouragement for trying the problems where uncertainty resides.

Going with the "gut instinct" is always the way to go when solving a problem. Second guessing should be avoided at all costs. Have confidence in the ability to do well.

For essay questions, create an outline in advance that will keep the mind organized and make certain that all of the points are remembered. For multiple choice, read every answer, even if the correct one has been spotted - a better one may exist.

Continue at a pace that is reasonable and not rushed, in order to be able to work carefully. Provide enough time to go over the answers at the end, to check for small errors that can be corrected.

Should a feeling of panic begin, breathe deeply, and think of the feeling of the body releasing sand through its pores. Visualize a calm, peaceful place, and include all of the sights, sounds and sensations of this image. Continue the deep breathing, and take a few minutes to continue this with closed eyes. When all is well again, return to the test.

If a "blanking" occurs for a certain question, skip it and move on to the next question. There will be time to return to the other question later. Get everything done that can be done, first, to guarantee all the grades that can be compiled, and to build all of the confidence possible. Then return to the weaker questions to build the marks from there.

Remember, one's own reality can be created, so as long as the belief is there, success will follow. And remember: anxiety can happen later, right now, there's an exam to be written!

After the examination is complete, whether there is a feeling for a good grade or a bad grade, don't dwell on the exam, and be certain to follow through on the reward that was promised...and enjoy it! Don't dwell on any mistakes that have been made, as there is nothing that can be done at this point anyway.

Additionally, don't begin to study for the next test right away. Do something relaxing for a while, and let the mind relax and prepare itself to begin absorbing information again.

From the results of the exam - both the grade and the entire experience, be certain to learn from what has gone on. Perfect studying habits and work some more on confidence in order to make the next examination experience even better than the last one.

Learn to avoid places where openings occurred for laziness, procrastination and day dreaming.

Use the time between this exam and the next one to better learn to relax, even learning to relax on cue, so that any anxiety can be controlled during the next exam. Learn how to relax the body. Slouch in your chair if that helps. Tighten and then relax all of the different muscle groups, one group at a time, beginning with the feet and then working all the way up to the neck and face. This will ultimately relax the muscles more than they were to begin with. Learn how to breathe deeply and comfortably, and focus on this breathing going in and out as a relaxing thought. With every exhale, repeat the word "relax."

As common as test anxiety is, it is very possible to overcome it. Make yourself one of the test-takers who overcome this frustrating hindrance.

Special Report: Retaking the Test: What Are Your Chances at Improving Your Score?

After going through the experience of taking a major test, many test takers feel that once is enough. The test usually comes during a period of transition in the test taker's life, and taking the test is only one of a series of important events. With so many distractions and conflicting recommendations, it may be difficult for a test taker to rationally determine whether or not he should retake the test after viewing his scores.

The importance of the test usually only adds to the burden of the retake decision. However, don't be swayed by emotion. There a few simple questions that you can ask yourself to guide you as you try to determine whether a retake would improve your score:

1. What went wrong? Why wasn't your score what you expected?

Can you point to a single factor or problem that you feel caused the low score? Were you sick on test day? Was there an emotional upheaval in your life that caused a distraction? Were you late for the test or not able to use the full time allotment? If you can point to any of these specific, individual problems, then a retake should definitely be considered.

2. Is there enough time to improve?

Many problems that may show up in your score report may take a lot of time for improvement. A deficiency in a particular math skill may require weeks or months of tutoring and studying to improve. If you have enough time to improve an identified weakness, then a retake should definitely be considered.

3. How will additional scores be used? Will a score average, highest score, or most recent score be used?

Different test scores may be handled completely differently. If you've taken the test multiple times, sometimes your highest score is used, sometimes your average score is computed and used, and sometimes your most recent score is used. Make sure you understand what method will be used to evaluate your scores, and use that to help you determine whether a retake should be considered.

4. Are my practice test scores significantly higher than my actual test score?

If you have taken a lot of practice tests and are consistently scoring at a much higher level than your actual test score, then you should consider a retake. However, if you've taken five practice tests and only one of your scores was higher than your actual test score, or if your practice test scores were only slightly higher than your actual test score, then it is unlikely that you will significantly increase your score.

5. Do I need perfect scores or will I be able to live with this score? Will this score still allow me to follow my dreams?

What kind of score is acceptable to you? Is your current score "good enough?" Do you have to have a certain score in order to pursue the future of your dreams? If you won't be happy with your current score, and there's no way that you could live with it, then you should consider a retake. However, don't get your hopes up. If you are looking for significant improvement, that may or may not be possible. But if you won't be happy otherwise, it is at least worth the effort.
Remember that there are other considerations. To achieve your dream, it is likely that your grades may also be taken into account. A great test score is usually not the only thing necessary to succeed. Make sure that you aren't overemphasizing the importance of a high test score.

Furthermore, a retake does not always result in a higher score. Some test takers will score lower on a retake, rather than higher. One study shows that one-fourth of test takers will achieve a significant improvement in test score, while one-sixth of test takers will actually show a decrease. While this shows that most test takers will improve, the majority will only improve their scores a little and a retake may not be worth the test taker's effort.

Finally, if a test is taken only once and is considered in the added context of good grades on the part of a test taker, the person reviewing the grades and scores may be tempted to assume that the test taker just had a bad day while taking the test, and may discount the low test score in favor of the high grades. But if the test is retaken and the scores are approximately the same, then the validity of the low scores are only confirmed. Therefore, a retake could actually hurt a test taker by definitely bracketing a test taker's score ability to a limited range.

Special Report: Additional Bonus Material

Due to our efforts to try to keep this book to a manageable length, we've created a link that will give you access to all of your additional bonus material.

Please visit http://www.mometrix.com/bonus948/staarg7write to access the information.